START A KNIFE SHARPENING SERVICE

A COMPREHENSIVE HOW-TO GUIDE

An easy, practical side-hustle to earn an extra **$10,000** or more every year.

KYLE KAPLAN

For permission requests, write to Kyle Kaplan, addressed "Attention: Permissions Coordinator,"
startasharpeningservice@gmail.com
https://startasharpeningservice.com/

Ordering Information: https://startasharpeningservice.com/

Quantity sales. Special discounts are available on quantity purchases by corporations, associations, and others. Orders by US trade bookstores and wholesalers. For details, contact the publisher at the address above.

Editing by The Pro Book Editor
Interior Design by IAPS.rocks
Cover Design by Amygdala Design

1. Main category—BUSINESS & ECONOMICS / Entrepreneurship
2. Other category—BUSINESS & ECONOMICS / Home-Based Businesses
3. Other category—BUSINESS & ECONOMICS / Freelance & Self-Employment

First Edition

TABLE OF CONTENTS

PREFACE

In October 2017, when I was twenty-seven years old, my girlfriend at the time and her two kids moved into my house, and my two roommates moved out. I became the children's pseudo-stepdad, and for the first time in my life, I was responsible for people other than just myself.

I instantly felt the weight of that responsibility, and the financial stress of the transition was brutal. Without my two roommates to help me pay the rent, I learned my income wasn't enough to support a family. I blew through my savings in the first three months. When the financial troubles set in, we quickly made budgets and trimmed the fat from our spending anywhere we could. I stopped going out to eat and stopped taking small vacations. I stopped going out for drinks with my friends, and I didn't buy a single new article of clothing for myself that year. Still, I struggled. Rent and utilities alone took more than half my income and combined with the rest of my expenses, I came up short almost every month.

After nearly a year of racking up debt, I reached a critical breaking point. I had maxed out all my credit cards, my bank accounts had negative balances, I had nothing of value to sell, and my whole next paycheck was already committed to keeping the roof over our heads. There were many nights that I simply couldn't afford a healthy dinner, so we ate mac 'n' cheese. My girlfriend was in the same position. She was working two part-time jobs, totaling thirty hours per week, because she needed to be available for her children after school. We weren't making enough money to get out of our hole, let alone get ahead, so we needed a creative solution to earn more. I needed a side hustle.

I live in Santa Fe, New Mexico. It's a lovely, medium-size city in the middle of the high-altitude desert. Santa Fe is a popular vacation and retirement destination, but only about 70,000 people live here full-time. Not being a large city, Santa Fe was a late adopter of many food delivery businesses like Postmates and Instacart, and I drove a two-door Jeep that wasn't suitable for Uber or Lyft. Because these opportunities were not available to me when I needed extra income, I had to figure something else out. In hindsight, I'm glad I had to find another solution to generate more income, because it led me to my sharpening service. I believe that as humans, we always adapt to our environments, and we discover creative solutions when we find ourselves in tough situations. If you are reading this book because you are looking for a creative and practical way to earn more money, you're in the right place.

I started my knife-sharpening service in November 2018. It took me two evenings to set up my website, register my business with Google and Yelp, and put ads in a local shopping center's newsletter. Within ten days, I had made more than $300! At that time in my life, an extra $300 was everything. My sharpening service, which I named Next Day Knife Sharpening Santa Fe, is small. I sharpen knives for about ten customers per week. I have very little overhead, so most of the money I make (after taxes) can go straight into my pocket. My time commitment to the business is about six to eight hours per week, and I make on average $800 to $1,200 per month. These aren't staggering numbers, but the money I made from my sharpening service was enough to pull me out of my financial hole and give me some breathing room.

You may be asking how I chose to start a knife-sharpening service, of all things. The answer is simple. For the past nine years, I have worked for a company that manufactures high-end knife-sharpening equipment, called Wicked Edge Precision Knife Sharpeners.

Wicked Edge sharpening equipment is professional grade, designed for both at-home knife enthusiasts and businesses. Many people, including me, regard Wicked Edge's sharpening systems to be the best sharpening equipment in the world. One of the primary components of my job at Wicked Edge is tech support, by which I help people learn how to use the sharpening equipment. I contribute to writing the company's instructional content. I teach people how the equipment works at various trade shows and give product training throughout the United States and sometimes overseas. I love what I do, and I love the company I work for. Clay Allison, the inventor of Wicked Edge and founder of the company, is my greatest mentor. He has taught me most of what I know about sharpening and about business.

I started working for Wicked Edge when I was twenty-one years old. At the time, there were just four of us who worked there, including the owner and his wife. Under Clay's leadership, and with a lot of hard work over the years, I have helped Wicked Edge grow into a great company with a brand known to knife enthusiasts worldwide. My experience working for Wicked Edge taught me what it takes to build an industry-leading company from the ground up. The thousands of hours I've spent talking to Wicked Edge customers has put me in the unique position of being able to speak with many other knife-sharpening-business owners about their sharpening services. I've learned a lot about the various strategies they've used to become successful in this business, and I have experienced firsthand what works and what doesn't. It's my goal to share that knowledge with you so you don't have to go through the trial and error that many of us in this business had to go through.

I wrote this book because I know how painful it can be to struggle with finances. I know what it feels like to choose between paying a bill and buying groceries. I know what it's like to turn friends down when they invite you to go do something fun, simply because you don't have enough gas in your car to get there. It's hard out there, and everyone needs an extra edge to get ahead. I want to help, and I believe I can because I became successful in this endeavor and I've spent my entire adult life teaching people how to sharpen knives. I'm confident that most of you who fully commit to starting a sharpening service will become successful because starting and operating a sharpening service isn't difficult. It takes a little time and dedication to get started, and then you'll be able to provide a better life for yourself and your family.

You must believe in yourself to start a business. Many people don't, which is why millions of people deliver food or gives rides for extra money. The fact that you're reading this book is proof that you have the correct dedication and desire to learn, and I'm grateful to be able to share my knowledge with you to help you become successful. There's something magical that happens within you when you become a small-business owner. The amount of pride and accomplishment I felt after launching my website and making my first sale is hard to describe. The confidence it instilled in me is something I will carry with me for the rest of my life. My ultimate goal for this book is to inspire other people to give themselves the gift of becoming a small-business owner. It will change your life forever.

INTRODUCTION

How many people do you know who have knives and use them? It's a fair assumption that every household has at least one knife, and most households have many knives. Knives are used for thousands of purposes every day. As one of mankind's oldest tools, they're an intricate part of our lives. I challenge you to keep a tally of each time you use a knife in a week and what you use it for. You'll find the results are probably much higher than you expected. Also, pay attention to how those knives performed. Did it feel like a hassle or a chore to cut something, or was it easy and satisfying?

Knives get dull when they're used, so they need to be maintained (sharpened), or they won't perform well. How frequently should they be sharpened? That entirely depends on how they were used, the quality of the prior sharpening job, the hardness of steel they are made from, and how well they were cared for between uses. On average, I recommend a bare minimum of twice a year, if the sharpening is done properly.

To understand the market potential on a macro scale: at a minimum of one knife per household, with 128 million households in the United States as of 2019, and assuming every household could be convinced to have their one knife sharpened twice per year at an average price of five dollars per sharpening, the market opportunity would be $1.28 billion annually in the United States alone.

When most people think of knives, they think kitchen knives. Though that's the largest market segment, it's far from the only one. There are also pocketknives, hunting knives, fishing knives, survival knives, tactical knives, rescue knives, collector knives, utility knives, and many more. To better understand how to position a profitable knife-sharpening business in the market, it's helpful to break the market down not just by knife type, but also by the personalities who use them.

This is a very basic list of who uses knives every day:

- home cooks and culinary enthusiasts
- chefs and line cooks
- warehouse workers
- construction workers
- electricians
- plumbers
- handymen
- gardeners
- police officers
- security guards
- fire fighters and rescue workers
- military personnel
- hunters
- commercial and recreational fishermen
- campers, backpackers, and outdoor enthusiasts
- knife collectors
- butchers
- movers
- woodworkers
- food packers
- farmers, ranchers, and agricultural workers

Knife use is everywhere, and as soon as you look for it, you'll see it as clear as day. The market potential for knife sharpening is huge. Your job, as the owner of a knife-sharpening service, is to unlock that potential. Throughout this book, I'll tell you about the ways to do that.

In the minds of many, sharpening knives and achieving great results requires the acquisition of knowledge and skills that can take years of practice and dedication to learn. I believe that used to be true, but it's not anymore. Sharpening equipment now exists that allows anyone to accomplish amazing results with relatively little practice. But if it's so easy, why doesn't everyone sharpen their own knives? Good sharpening equipment is cost prohibitive to most people who only want their knives sharpened a few times a year, and it also requires learning how to use it—a skill most people don't wish to devote the time and energy into developing. Like I said, it's not hard, but there is a slight learning curve, and it takes a bit of practice. During the nine years I've spent working at Wicked Edge Precision Knife Sharpeners, and from the approximately 10,000 knives I've sharpened, I've developed a system for using this equipment that's effective, efficient, repeatable, and teachable. I will share that system with you in this book. How long will it take you to become proficient with the sharpening equipment? After practicing on fifteen to twenty knives and following the training plan outlined in the second half of this book, you'll be confident in your ability to produce amazing results.

There are two components of this book: (1) starting and operating a small knife-sharpening business, and (2) the nuts-and-bolts technical aspect of knife sharpening. Throughout part one, you'll learn the main sharpening-service business strategies that people use in this industry, marketing strategies I have found to be successful, and learn a step-by-step plan that you can use to start your small knife-sharpening business. Though there are several knife-sharpening-service business models, most of this book will be about the strategy that I know works. I'll also describe the other models, and which aspects of those models make them appealing in specific scenarios. Part two of this book is about how to sharpen knives efficiently and effectively.

PART ONE

- six different business models and strategies for sharpening services that you can choose from to start your business
- a step-by-step plan for how to launch your business, including tips for building your website, how to set your pricing, and setting up payment methods
- how to market your sharpening service to attract customers and how to build a great reputation
- information about finances and taxes
- how to stay organized and protect your customers' knives

PART TWO

- the basic principles of knife edges and sharpening
- an overview of different sharpening equipment and which products to choose for your sharpening service
- how knife-sharpening equipment works and how to use it
- how to make observations about knives and determine how to sharpen them

- a step-by-step training guide to slash the learning curve and become proficient with the sharpening equipment very quickly
- a breakdown of common blade types and how to sharpen them, and information about sharpening less common blade types

After reading this book and following some simple steps, you'll have the ability to create for yourself a side income that equals approximately $10,000 or more every year. You'll be able to take some of the financial stress out of your life or put more money into savings, and you can do it in your own time. This book is primarily about starting a sharpening service as a side business. However, if you want to start a full-time sharpening business, or you already own or work for a sharpening service and you're seeking new ideas, you'll also find the content of this book useful.

The best part about sharpening knives compared to delivering food or giving rides for extra income is that you can be on your own schedule *and* you can make significantly more money per hour. You can sit down in the evening, sharpen a couple knives, get up and make dinner, go for a walk, play with your kids or help them with their homework, and then sharpen a couple more knives. You don't have to be on someone else's time.

Starting a small business of your own does take more effort than driving for Uber or Lyft, so before you begin this journey, it's important to ask yourself why you want to start a small business. You need to understand your motivation. This business is one of the easiest to start and operate, but it takes some dedication and commitment to become successful. There will be times when you become tired, discouraged, or simply lose your drive. When those times come, it's helpful to dig deep and remember exactly why you decided to start a business. The motivation to start a business can come in many forms. The most common motivator when people start businesses is money. Though that is a good enough reason to start a small business, it's vague.

Try to describe what you'll do with the extra income you'll produce when your business becomes successful. Will you use this income for a down payment on a house? Put money away for your children's college education? Travel? Repay debt? Are you a student seeking a solution to earn money without being away from your friends and studies for too long? Are you retired and looking for a way to supplement your fixed income? Or do you have nonfinancial motivations? Do you want to offer something of value to your community? Are you passionate about knives, or an aspiring knife maker looking for a way to learn about sharpening and make a side income while you're at it? Or are you simply looking to gain experience in starting a small business so you can apply this experience to a larger endeavor later? Whatever drives you, I encourage you to think hard about your goals and write them down. Be very specific.

The most important piece of advice I can offer to those of you who are starting your first business is this: always remember that you have the absolute right to give this to yourself, and you deserve it. You can do this. Nothing or no one can stop you, nor do they have the right to get in your way. Give yourself the life you want to have because you deserve to create that life for yourself.

Starting a business will change you. It will change the way you view the world. You'll start seeing opportunities in more places, and you'll develop the courage and the confidence to chase them. Before I started my sharpening service, I often felt defeated. I felt like I was at the mercy of everyone else, and there wasn't much I could do to change that. After I started my business and put in the work to make it successful, I felt a sense of accomplishment and satisfaction that I had never felt before. This feeling alone is why I recommend starting a small business instead of one of the more common side-hustle jobs available today, like Uber or Postmates. You'll develop skills and obtain knowledge that you can apply to future businesses and many other parts of your life, and you'll find the work far more rewarding.

I don't believe in get-rich-quick schemes. I despise them. I prefer practical, applicable, and actionable strategies for building success. All you need to do is make a plan and have the discipline and dedication to stick to it. Throughout this book, you'll find step-by-step checklists so you can learn how to focus your efforts and keep your plan on track. When you think about starting a business, it can seem daunting. But when you can break down all that's required into small groups of specific tasks, the overall path to success becomes more clear and less intimidating. If at any point you feel overwhelmed as you're getting your business started, take a step back and refer to one of the to-do lists provided in this book, or make your own list. Make it as detailed as possible. If something needs to be done, even a task as minor as sending an email, put it on the list. One of the greatest motivators for me is the gratification of completing tasks. As you cross items off your list, I guarantee you'll find motivation to move on to the next one.

When starting a small business, it's important to understand your risks. You should consider all the things you stand to lose if you fail. Fortunately, there's not much to lose if you fail at starting a small sharpening service. Once you've identified your risk factors, create a plan to mitigate them. For instance, your sharpening equipment will be your most expensive investment. If you fail, you may be able to return or resell that equipment to recoup a lot of your cash. Or you can keep it and sharpen knives for yourself, your family, and your friends for the rest of your life. One of the most important things to consider when managing risk is the upside of failure. Even if you fail within the first four weeks, what will you have gained? Failure is one of the best teaching experiences, and through it you'll gain experience, knowledge, and skills you can apply to your next venture. In my sincere opinion, it's better to try something and fail than to miss out on an opportunity by never trying at all.

Before moving on to the next chapter, I encourage you to take some time to write down all your goals. Be very specific about them. Be realistic but be ambitions. What do you hope to gain from starting a knife-sharpening business?

PART 1
KNIFE-SHARPENING BUSINESS STRATEGIES

CHAPTER 1

GETTING STARTED

TO START A SHARPENING SERVICE, you'll need some start-up cash, a vehicle or other form of transportation, a computer with internet connection, a smartphone, and a desk or table. To operate your sharpening service to generate a side income of $10,000 per year, be prepared to spend three to five hours per week sharpening knives and one to two hours per week at your computer doing marketing, customer service, and some occasional light accounting work. If you use either the delivery or mobile-sharpening-service business models, which will be described later in this chapter, be prepared to spend a few hours per week driving.

The exact amount of money you'll need to get your business started will vary depending on the business model you choose to build. You also don't have to make all your purchases at once. You can start small and grow your business over time, as you begin to generate income. At a minimum, you'll need approximately $500 to get started to pay for your sharpening equipment and some other miscellaneous items that are necessities, all of which will be outlined in detail throughout this book. To build an exact replica of the business model I created, it will cost you approximately $1,200. Twelve hundred dollars is a significant amount of money to invest, but your business can pay you back tenfold in your first year if you apply the right amount of focus and determination in building it.

To get started, the first aspect to consider is your strategy. These are the basic factors to consider:

- What will be your days and hours of operation?
- How will you find your customers?

- How will you collect knives from your customers?
- When and where will you sharpen the knives?
- How will your customers receive their sharpened knives?

First, start by identifying how much time and exactly which time blocks you have available to dedicate to your sharpening service. The time you have available will impact the strategy you create. I work my regular job from 8:00 a.m. to 4:00 p.m., Monday through Friday, so I had to set up my service so it could be operational in the evenings and on weekends. If you work nights, you may need to develop a different strategy than I used. Draw out a calendar that shows exactly which time blocks you have available.

Next, compare these time blocks to the times when customers are available. For instance, most people don't like conducting business before 8:00 a.m. and after 7:00 p.m. Does the time you have fit into that window? If your available time does not fall between 8:00 a.m. and 7:00 p.m., you'll need to develop a strategy that involves not being present for knife transactions, or focusing your service on days you have off from your other job(s).

Once you've figured out your schedule, you can start to develop a plan for how you'll conduct transactions. Will you ask your customers to come to you? Or will you go to your customers? There are six strategies that I have seen sharpening services use for conducting transactions:

1. Immediate-sharpening service
2. Drop-off/pickup location service
3. Pickup and delivery service
4. Mail-in service
5. Knife-exchange service
6. Mobile sharpening service

1. IMMEDIATE-SHARPENING-SERVICE STRATEGY

The immediate-sharpening-service strategy is excellent for attracting new customers. This strategy is very simple. Set up your sharpening equipment in public view and let people bring you their knives. Sharpen the knives immediately for the customer. Once the knives have been sharpened for a customer, the customer pays you, takes his or her knives, and leaves. If you plan to use this strategy, set up your sharpener in places where the people who use knives more often are concentrated. These locations are ideal:

- grocery stores
- farmers markets
- hardware stores
- shooting ranges
- gun or knife shows
- outdoor retailer locations
- fishing marinas
- kitchen-supply stores
- restaurant-supply stores

To set up your sharpener at one of these locations, you'll need to coordinate with the managers of these properties. Some will be open to the idea, and some won't. You may need to rent the space that you use, which can sometimes be costly. Never set up a sharpener in a public place or in front of a business without consulting with the property manager first.

The immediate-sharpening-service strategy will require some patience to get started. After you've found a location willing to host you and negotiated how much you'll pay for using the space, you'll need to show up consistently so people get used to seeing you there. Set a schedule and stick to it. Once people see you there a few times and talk to you, they'll be more likely to remember to bring their knives to you. If you fail to show up during your usual time slot, people may see you as unreliable and decide to not bring knives with them the next time they visit that location. Before committing to a location or time, make sure you can easily fit it into your schedule. If you feel that commitment will overburden you, don't make the commitment and develop a different strategy for your knife-sharpening service.

Pocketknives are easy to capitalize on at immediate-sharpening locations simply because they're usually in someone's pocket and not in a drawer at home. Train yourself to look for the knife clip on the outside of people's pockets. If you see someone is carrying a pocketknife, ask him or her if you can sharpen it.

It's helpful to create a sign or a banner for your service that has the name of your service, the service you offer, and your pricing on it. Have your banner professionally printed. It will only cost you twenty to forty dollars to have it printed.

Before committing to a time slot and location, analyze your potential financial risk. For instance, if the retail location or farmers market requests $100 per day to set up at their location, calculate how many knives you need to sharpen that day to break even, and then how many you need to sharpen on top of that to make your profit goal for the day. If you only have one day a week to dedicate to sharpening and your goal is to profit $250 per week, you may wish to choose a venue that doesn't cost so much in rent. If you're charging seven dollars per knife and want to make $250 profit after you pay the $100 in rent for the table space, you would need to sharpen fifty knives to hit your goal. It's doable, but you'll need to focus on developing relationships with customers, collecting email addresses, and sending reminders so customers remember to bring their knives to the market.

Farmers markets usually charge between $20 and $100 to rent table space. But you can sometimes negotiate with retail business managers for lower or even zero cost to you because your service could be beneficial to them. Your presence in their businesses provides a service to their customers that the business doesn't have to pay for. Customers will like that they can get their knives sharpened and shop at the same time, and sometimes, they'll stay shopping longer while they wait for you to finish their knives. It's very possible that your sharpening service will even bring new customers into the business that's hosting you. Talk this through when you're negotiating rates at retail businesses.

Shooting ranges are interesting, especially public shooting ranges, because almost everyone who frequents these places carries pocketknives. Gun owners can be what people call "gear junkies." These people love to collect gear, including knives. It's been said that "not everyone who's into knives has a gun, but everyone who's into guns carries a knife." From my experience, that's usually true. If you set up your sharpener at a public shooting range for an afternoon on a weekend, you can make some decent money at very little cost to you by sharpening people's pocketknives. Just make sure to bring ear protection and set up your sharpener so it's not in people's way.

2. DROP-OFF/PICKUP LOCATION SHARPENING-SERVICE STRATEGY

There are two types of drop-off/pickup locations, which I call a manned location and an unmanned location. Drop-off/pickup business models are appealing because you can sharpen knives in your free time at home, as opposed to immediate sharpening where you're away from home and your everyday life activities for larger blocks of time.

A manned location takes advantage of a place where people will be, like a retail location, and asks the business owner and the employees to help you with your service. I experimented with this type of service at my stepdad's hardware store. We built a simple box with shelving for multiple bins to store knives. Customers would come in, leave their knives, and I would pick the knives up after I got out of work. I would then sharpen them at home and deliver them back to the hardware store, where the customers could pick them up, the next day.

I created a form for customers to fill out. This form included the customer's name, address, phone number, email, and a space in which they could list their knives. You can find a sample of this form at the end of chapter 6. With this information, I knew exactly who the knives belonged to and how to contact that person if there was any sort of issue. Customers were instructed to fill out the form when they dropped off their knives and to place the form in the bin with their knives.

The problem with this strategy was it required training the employees at the hardware store in how the system worked. Those employees would also have to interact with the customers and guide them through the system. This wouldn't have been possible if I weren't family with the business owner because it was disruptive to the everyday activities of the business. If you know someone who has a small retail business at a great location, ask that person if he or she would like to help you. You may be able to work a deal where you pay the business a fixed amount or a percentage of revenue each month. If the person is a close friend or family member, he or she may help you out for no cost. If you do find someone who's willing to help, you can sharpen his or her knives regularly for free.

The unmanned approach to drop-off/pickup locations can be very convenient because no third party is involved. But this isn't as easy to set up as it may sound. There is a big risk involved. Knives can get stolen, mishandled, or mixed up. Protecting your customers' knives should always be your top priority in this business. The only way I've seen this done effectively is with custom-built lockboxes.

If you plan to build lockboxes, make sure they are very secure. People's knife collections can be worth many hundreds of dollars. Lockboxes work well if you use combination locks. Ideally, the box has multiple individual slots for knives, and each slot has its own lock. Try to build the box out of metal, not wood, and make sure it's secured very well to the ground or find another solution to be sure the whole box won't get stolen. Make a permanent sign on the box that says "Knife Sharpening" to attract attention to the box, and make sure your contact information and website can be found easily on the box. A great way to make sure customers get to your website is to use a QR code on the lockbox that people can scan from their phones.

Before you build your box(es), make sure you have a place to put them. Again, this may require negotiating with business owners. You can put a lockbox in front of your house, and that might be the easiest solution, but it only works if you live in a convenient location. It's unlikely that people will want to use your sharpening service if they must drive ten miles outside of town to drop off and pick up their knives.

If you decide to use lockboxes and have a strategy in place for where to locate them, the next piece of the puzzle is making sure your customers know how to use them. You'll need to devise an ordering system so customers can contact you to place their orders. When a customer contacts you, you'll need to provide the combination to the lock for a specific numbered slot in the box where the customer can leave his or her knives. Then provide the pickup instructions and payment instructions. For redundancy, it's helpful to leave a paper order form waiting for the customer at the box to fill out and leave with their knives, so you will know who the knives belong to and how to contact each person. You'll need to devise a tracking system to know which combinations you've given to which customers and which slots and combinations are currently in use. That way you don't accidentally give the same slot and lock combination to multiple active customers.

If you have multiple lockboxes scattered throughout your city or neighborhood, make sure to include a map or the addresses of their locations on your website so your customers can find the lockbox that's most convenient for them to use. One of the great advantages about using multiple lockboxes is that it greatly increases your exposure, and more people will learn about your sharpening service, especially if you can put them in popular places.

3. PICKUP AND DELIVERY SHARPENING-SERVICE STRATEGY

Though I do some immediate sharpening successfully, and I have experimented with a drop box at a local business and had success, the pickup and delivery model is by far my preference for how to conduct my sharpening service. This model is how I built my sharpening business. It's very convenient for customers, and I've found that making things convenient for customers plays a large part in becoming successful in business. The pickup and delivery model works very well when you live in a medium-to-large-size city. If you live in a rural area where houses are very spread apart (several miles between them) the immediate or drop-off/pickup models might be better for you.

The way a pickup and delivery sharpening service works is by asking customers to schedule orders in advance and asking them to provide you with their contact information and address. Then plan a pickup and delivery route each day based on the sharpened knives that need to be delivered and the new orders you have scheduled for that day. If you plan your route well, it won't take a lot of time. Once you complete your route for the day, sharpen knives at home in your leisure time. This is a great model for people who need to have flexible schedules because of kids, recreational activities, or miscellaneous life stuff that just seems to come up every day.

When considering this type of business model, you should refer to the scheduled time you set aside for your sharpening service. Many people aren't home before 5:30 in the afternoon, and usually people don't want to conduct business while they're eating dinner. Not to mention, they'll probably want their knives back earlier in the evening so they can cook dinner. So the optimum pickup/delivery time window is in the early evening. There's also a brief window in the morning before people leave for work. That window is from 7:30 to 8:30 a.m. Weekends are great because people are often home on the weekends, so you can offer a more flexible pickup and delivery schedule.

It's helpful to contact your customers before you begin driving to make sure they're available. Sometimes, people will forget about the order they placed with you and run out on an errand during their scheduled pickup or delivery time. It's an enormous waste of your time and gas to go to a destination where no one is home.

If you run late, call your customers and inform them of the delay. People are usually understanding, and they will think more highly of you if you simply call ahead and tell them you're running a little late. The opposite is true if you're late and don't call ahead. If you're late and don't call ahead, your customer may see you as unreliable and not order from you again. In the pickup and delivery business, punctuality and proactive communications are crucial for developing lasting relationships with your customers. Always keep a list of your customer's phone numbers and addresses with you as you make your delivery route and make sure you have a healthy charge on your phone battery before you start driving.

There's no such thing as a knife emergency, so don't rush. It's okay to be a little late sometimes if you call ahead, and it sure beats an accident or speeding ticket. A $70 speeding ticket will take your profits from your business that day, and a car accident can bring your new business to a grinding stop. Or worse yet, you could hurt someone or yourself. It's just not worth it. Think long term and protect yourself, your community, and your business. Don't rush.

4. MAIL-IN SHARPENING-SERVICE STRATEGY

This strategy is one of the more complicated to set up and requires significantly more marketing. It works by having customers ship their knives to you. Once the knives have been sharpened, accept payment electronically and then ship the knives back to the customer. The mail-in strategy is appealing to some people because they can market their service to everyone in the country—they aren't limited to smaller markets that are restricted by geography.

I've seen this done successfully in two ways: focus on very high volume and low prices, or focus on prime quality sharpening with very high prices.

The high-volume/low-price strategy requires keeping your sharpening costs and prices low to outbid local sharpening services.

The high-quality/high-price strategy focuses on customers who have a deep passion about their knives and own very expensive cutlery. Sharpening services that cater to these types of people take their share of the market by advertising a higher quality, more precision-oriented sharpening job than local services, and they spend a lot of time investing in their reputation as a superior sharpening service.

There are two restrictive issues for either of the mail-in service strategies. The first is the time it takes for knives to be in transit. It's my experience that people don't want to wait around a week or more for their knives to be sharpened and returned to them. The second is the shipping cost. At a minimum, shipping will cost about ten dollars round trip, and usually higher than that. If a local service is offering a price of five dollars per knife and a customer has four knives sharpened, the total price will be twenty dollars plus tax. Even if the mail-in sharpening service can sharpen knives for three dollars each, with ten dollars in shipping costs, the customer will pay twenty-three dollars total. That means to outbid the local service, the mail-in service needs to charge bottom-dollar and maximize the number of knives they sharpen per customer to reduce the per-knife shipping cost. Or the mail-in service needs to offer a "better" sharpening solution than local services can offer and attract customers who want their expensive knives sharpened by a "superior" sharpening service. If knife enthusiasts who own expensive cutlery believe the mail-in service can take better care of their knives than the local service, it's possible higher prices and shipping costs won't discourage them.

In addition to shipping costs being prohibitive, the other factor that can make these services more undesirable than local services is the reliability of shipping carriers. If you ship enough packages, eventually, one will get lost, and the sharpening service could be responsible for replacing the lost knives. Shipping carriers offer shipping insurance for exactly this reason, but they often charge an additional fee for insuring packages.

The amount of marketing required to run a successful mail-in service is substantially more than required to run a local sharpening service. Not only does the mail-in service have to reach people around the country, but also it needs to convince them the service is trustworthy. To do this, a lot of digital content would need to be created and broadcast across many online platforms and a lot of marketing dollars pumped in to place advertisements in front of people on various platforms nationwide.

With all these factors making mail-in services seem undesirable compared to a locally-based sharpening-service model, especially for a part-time sharpening business, there's one way I've found the mail-in service strategy can benefit a part-time sharpening service. After you've spent time and energy investing in and building a loyal customer base and you've developed relationships with your customers, you may decide to move to a new city. If you do, it would be a lot of hard work wasted if your entire customer list becomes worthless to you. Instead of starting over, it may be helpful to reach out to your customers and ask if they would like to continue having their knives sharpened by you. If you have a strong relationship with them, they may be willing to take on the additional shipping costs to keep having their knives sharpened by you.

If you decide to create a mail-in sharpening service, you'll need the following:

- accounts with shipping carriers like USPS, UPS, or FedEx
- shipping software, like ShipStation
- boxes and packing materials to ship knives safely

It would also be helpful if you were able to set up a website that is capable of taking orders, collecting payment, and emailing shipping labels to customers automatically when they place their orders. This will be complicated to set up and could be expensive. The other way to make this work is simply to ask your customers to ship their knives to you by going to their local post office, UPS store, or FedEx store and then collecting payment by sending a PayPal invoice or Venmo money request after the knives have been sharpened. The latter solution is sloppier but will be less expensive and less complicated to get started.

5. KNIFE-EXCHANGE SHARPENING-SERVICE STRATEGY

The knife-exchange strategy works best for sharpening services that focus heavily on sharpening for businesses, like restaurants. This service involves exchanging dull knives for sharp knives. It is ideal for customers who cannot be without their knives for an extended period because their knives are part of their business operations. This strategy was mainly created for restaurants, as they cannot be without their knives for long.

The way the knife-exchange sharpening service works is for there to be two complete sets of knives. One set of knives stays at the restaurant, and the other set stays with the sharpening service. Periodically, depending on the time frame that has been agreed upon by both parties, the sharpening service will deliver sharp knives to the business and pick up the dull knives.

Most knife-exchange services ask the restaurant to carry the cost of the two sets of knives. This can be done in one of two ways:

1. The restaurant simply buys a second set of knives.
2. The restaurant pays a deposit to the sharpening service, and then the sharpening service purchases the knives.

If asking for a deposit, you can make it be refundable upon termination of the relationship, or the deposit can be nonrefundable. I've seen it done both ways. This is how it would work if the business relationship is terminated:

- Refundable deposit—The sharpening service would return the deposit to the restaurant but take out any necessary money to cover the cost of any knives that were damaged or lost. The knives would be returned to the sharpening service.
- Nonrefundable deposit—The sharpening service would return all the knives to the restaurant and keep the deposit.

It makes sense for the restaurant to carry the cost of the knives, as the knives will be used regularly by many different people. There is a high chance the knives will be damaged or lost while at the restaurant. If the restaurant buys into the sharpening service or pays a deposit, there will usually be an annual or biannual assessment of the knives and a renewal fee or a reduction in a refundable deposit is charged by the sharpening service to cover the cost of any knives that need to be replaced. The annual assessment is also a time to get feedback from the restaurant about how they think the sharpening service is performing.

There are two big advantages to a knife-exchange-service strategy. The first is you can sharpen knives in your free time if you have them ready by the agreed delivery time. The second is steady, reliable income. Once you've agreed on pricing and delivery frequency, you'll have created a guaranteed income source for yourself, provided you keep up with your end of the bargain and the business doesn't terminate the agreement for an unforeseeable reason like a business closure.

To set up the business model that asks the restaurant to pay a deposit so you can purchase knives, the first step is to create your sales pitch. To do that, you'll need to research several different knife-brand options for the restaurant to choose from. It's helpful to provide low-, medium-, and high-quality knife options. Buy some samples of the knives so the business can try them out in person. This will help them make their decision. Put together a brochure that displays the knives the business can choose from and display the cost per knife. Remember to double your prices, because you'll need to purchase two matching sets of knives. For instance, if the business wants four eight-inch chef's knives, you'll need to purchase eight of them. After the business has chosen its knife options, the total price of all the knives will be the initial deposit amount.

To select the knife options you'll offer to businesses, you may find it helpful to call or visit one or several restaurant-supply stores. Ask them which knives are their best sellers and build a list. You can purchase the knives from the restaurant-supply stores, or you can try contacting the knife manufacturers directly. You may be able to get a better price if you go directly to the manufacturers. Ask them what their minimum purchase amount is to qualify for wholesale pricing. It may be worth it for you to purchase knives in bulk, though you would have to carry the cost until you sign new business clients. I don't recommend purchasing knives in bulk until your business is well off the ground and you've proven your strategy works.

If the business already prefers a specific brand of knives that's not in your offerings, go online and find out how you can order those knives. If you can't find an easy way to order them, it may be best to simply ask the restaurant to purchase them and not pay a deposit. If the business already has one set of knives that's in good condition, that's great. Only one set of knives would need to be purchased to match it, and you can cut the deposit price for the restaurant in half. If you go this route, make sure to inspect the restaurant's knives in person before you agree to this. Their knives could be in very rough shape, which will take a lot of effort to fix. In that scenario, it's better for both parties to just replace the knives that are in poor condition and buy two new sets of knives.

After you've agreed with your client on the knives and the deposit price, the next factor to negotiate is the frequency of delivery. Again, it's helpful to come prepared with options the business can choose from. When planning out options for yourself, establish the minimum you would like to be paid per knife sharpened. That way you know what your bottom line is for negotiations. Then build out a formula that you can use to calculate the per-knife cost multiplied by the total number of knives, multiplied by the monthly frequency. It's better for you to sharpen more frequently, so you might consider adding a discount for each additional exchange period in a month. The formulas would look like this:

Option 1: (Total knives) x (price per knife) x (1 exchange per month)

Option 2: (Total knives) x (price per knife) x (2 exchanges per month) - (5% discount)

Option 3: (Total knives) x (price per knife) x (4 exchanges per month) - (10% discount)

I highly recommend putting all of your options and pricing together in an organized printed or digitalized presentation. The more professional you look, the more inclined businesses will be to work with you.

When sharpening knives for businesses, don't expect they'll hand you cash at each delivery. You'll need to set up a payment schedule and provide the business with an invoice for each billing period. In my experience, most businesses prefer to make monthly payments. Mail the customer an invoice or deliver it in person each month. More about pricing your sharpening services, payment methods, and invoicing will be covered in detail in the next chapter.

As a sales tactic, you may find it helpful to let the business try out some knives that you've sharpened. Try providing the business with a half-dozen knives to use for a few days to a week, and after the trial period is over, collect your knives and ask how they performed. Letting the business try out knives that you own gives you a great reason to schedule a second meeting to collect your knives, and the business will see firsthand what your service can do for them.

When working with businesses, punctuality and reliability are key. Try to be as close to on time as you can be. Businesses use their knives throughout their operational hours, so it's helpful to exchange knives before the business starts their workday or after they close for the day. Make sure you remind the business about their scheduled exchange in advance. Get the email addresses for two people on the business's staff and send them an email one day in advance to remind them you'll be there the next day to exchange knives. The business will need to collect the knives from the various areas throughout the business where they are stored, and it will save you time if the knives are collected before you arrive. I recommend acquiring the email addresses of two people on staff for redundancy. If one of those people has a day off or is out sick, you'll be covered.

Sharpening for businesses using a knife-exchange strategy comes with more requirements and liabilities than sharpening for households and individuals. You'll need to keep excellent records of transactions and keep a tally of the knives the business purchased with their deposit. It's helpful to keep a log sheet of knife exchanges. Record the number of knives that are exchanged each time with the date they were exchanged. Ask a representative from the company to sign the log each time. That way, if a knife is missing when you pick up knives, the business won't blame you for losing it. If a knife is misplaced or damaged while it's in your possession, you'll be financially responsible. If you've asked the business to pay a nonrefundable deposit, they own the knives. Always remember that and carefully protect the knives

If asking for deposits and keeping very accurate records seems like it could be too much work for you, there is another option. You could buy the knives yourself and not ask the business to pay a deposit. This could end up costing you hundreds of dollars per business customer, but you would have more flexibility. If you do it this way, you could try charging more per sharpening on each knife. However, there will also be the cost of replacing lost or damaged knives and chasing down businesses for reimbursement isn't always easy.

6. MOBILE-SHARPENING-SERVICE STRATEGY

A mobile sharpening service takes advantage of several of the sharpening-service strategies discussed in this chapter. Primarily, a mobile sharpening service aims to go to its customers and sharpen knives immediately, without having to collect the knives and deliver them later. Mobile sharpeners frequently set up their sharpening stations in public, but also travel to businesses and households. This strategy will keep you away from your home life more than other strategies will, but you can cut your costs by not having to make a second trip to deliver knives.

To start a mobile sharpening service, you'll need a portable sharpening station. You can purchase a portable table and chair to set up wherever you plan to sharpen knives, or you can use a more creative solution. I've heard of a mobile sharpening service that attached its sharpening system to a bicycle and rigged up two support arms on each side of the bicycle that folded down and extended to the ground to add stability for sharpening. I have also witnessed sharpening stations set up in the back of vans and attached to the tailgates of pickup trucks.

If you plan on sharpening at multiple locations each day or each week, I highly recommend posting the days and times you will be at each location on your website. If you plan to go to people's homes or businesses to sharpen knives, make sure you devise a system for people to schedule sharpening in advance, and make your customers aware of the times you are available.

When sharpening for businesses, you can go to each business, set your sharpener up outside of the business somewhere that you don't interfere with customers, and sharpen all the business's knives without ever taking them away from the business's location. If you go to a business in the middle of its workday, I suggest you sharpen knives in batches so the business still has knives to use while you're sharpening.

DEVELOP A STRATEGY FOR YOU AND YOUR CUSTOMERS

When choosing a strategy, find a balance that works for both you and your customers. In the knife-sharpening business, convenience is key. For most people, knives are not the number one priority in their lives, but they do appreciate sharp knives compared to dull knives. Most people will not go far out of their way to have them sharpened, so make sure your service provides a convenient solution. However, don't overburden yourself. Test a strategy you think would work for both you and your customers and then make small changes to improve it as you learn. My sharpening service utilizes a combination of several of the strategies listed in this chapter, mainly focusing on the pickup/delivery model because it's the easiest for me to fit into my lifestyle, but it didn't start off that way. I had to find creative solutions and adapt to both my needs and the needs of my customers until I'd developed a strategy that worked.

For example, there's a large subdivision with about 2,500 upper-middle-class homes ten miles from where I live. I started marketing my services to the people in that area, knowing that I would likely be successful in finding new clients. My problem was that I found it too time-consuming to make pickups and deliveries to that area, and I was spending too much on gas. I found a local shopping center that allowed me to sharpen knives at their property. The shopping center didn't charge me for using their space, and I could come and go as I pleased. When I received orders from customers in the subdivision, I picked up the knives from each of my customers in that area and took them with me to the nearby shopping center. I set up my sharpening equipment and sharpened the knives in view of all the patrons. People approached me because they were curious about what I was doing, and I handed out business cards to each person I talked to. When I finished sharpening, I delivered the knives back to my customers.

SHARPENING FOR BUSINESSES

Business clients, like restaurants and butcher shops, can be very attractive to sharpening services because they have many knives that need frequent sharpening—meaning more income for you. However, there's a reason that you may wish to avoid making agreements with business, and that is your time commitment. If you make an agreement with a business to sharpen their knives on a set schedule, you'll be committed. Once you're locked into an agreement, you may have a hard time doing things like going out of town on vacation for a week. If you need a flexible schedule, you might choose to avoid making commitments to businesses. It wouldn't be difficult to contact one business and ask if you can sharpen their knives at an earlier or later date that month, but if you have many business clients, you could find yourself in hot water. If you're operating a sharpening service as a side job, I recommend making yourself known to businesses in your area and asking them to contact you on a needs basis when their knives get dull instead of creating a predetermined sharpening schedule with them. If you're operating a full-time sharpening service, I recommend capitalizing on business clients as much as possible by agreeing on a set sharpening schedule so you can create a steady, reliable revenue stream for your business.

E-COMMERCE

There are pros and cons to creating an e-commerce platform for a sharpening service, where customers may place orders and pay for your service on your website via electronic payment methods like credit cards, PayPal, or Apply Pay. E-commerce platforms are usually designed for selling hard goods. A customer places an order, pays for the item at the time of purchase, and the company delivers or ships the item to the customer. With service businesses, payment is usually collected after a job is complete because there are multiple factors that go into determining the final price. As a sharpening service operating an e-commerce platform, you would need to ask your customers to predetermine the number of knives they would like to have sharpened and select that quantity on your website, and then pay for your service in advance. In my experience, this is not a great solution. My reasons are as follows: Customers frequently miscount the number of knives they would like to have sharpened. Knives sometimes need extra, billable work like fixing a broken tip. Sometimes, customers will give you knives that you may not be able to sharpen, like a serrated bread knife. When these situations come up, there will be a discrepancy in the final price compared to the price the customer originally paid, and you would need to rebill the customer or refund the customer for the difference in price. This could create an accounting nightmare, and in my opinion, it's not worth the hassle for a small sharpening service.

However, there are a few benefits to e-commerce solutions for sharpening services. When done properly, e-commerce solutions can make ordering more convenient for your customers. In some scenarios, e-commerce can also save you time because you can automate your accounting and payment collection processes. For this to work correctly, find an e-commerce solution that allows for delayed payments, stores credit card information at the time of the purchase, and allows you to manually adjust the price and process the payment when you've completed the job. To protect their customers, many e-commerce website platforms don't allow this flexibility because of the liabilities presented by keeping credit card information on file and allowing business owners or employees to adjust prices and collect payment for any price they choose. Finding an e-commerce solution to meet the needs of a small service-type business will be difficult and likely expensive. In my opinion, the only sharpening service model that e-commerce is beneficial to is the mail-in service strategy.

BE FLEXIBLE AND OPEN TO CHANGE

The world is constantly evolving and changing, as are the needs and demands from customers. Twenty years ago, the mail-in-sharpening-service strategy would have been very difficult to make successful because internet marketing and e-commerce services weren't yet fully developed. Always be on the lookout for ways to improve and adapt to changing environments. Don't be afraid to make changes to your strategy as you go. For instance, it may be beneficial to start out using the immediate-sharpening-service strategy to develop new customers and collect email addresses, but after you meet enough people, you may decide to switch to a pickup and delivery sharpening service strategy, which would keep you away from your home life for shorter blocks of time.

A STRATEGY THAT WORKS

You can use any of the strategies discussed in this chapter, or a combination of them, to earn an income of $10,000 or more a year. Remember: all you need to do is find ten customers per week to be successful. It's up to you to determine which business model may be the best choice for you and your lifestyle. If you wish to create a business that's easy to launch, this is how I recommend using the strategies outlined in this chapter. Start your business using simple tactics and then grow it if you feel the desire to make your business larger.

Start with either the pickup and delivery business model, immediate-sharpening-service model, or mobile-sharpening-service model. Any of the three will be easy to get started. The delivery model will be very convenient for both you and your customers, whereas the immediate model is better to attract new customers. You can use a combination of these business models, which is exactly what I did to start my sharpening service.

After you've created a sizable customer base and a good reputation, try expanding your service by using the drop-off/pickup business model. Find some locations where you can place drop boxes for knives. You can build the drop boxes yourself or hire someone to build them for you. Drop-off/pickup locations will allow your service to be more visible and more available to more people, and you'll save time visiting these knife collection points compared to driving to each customer's house.

If you want to continue to grow your business, develop some business clients, like restaurants. You can try the mobile-sharpening-service strategy and sharpen knives at the restaurant, or you can use the knife-exchange strategy.

If you want to take your business nationally, invest in digital marketing and start offering a mail-in option to people all around the country.

The business methods and marketing tactics described in the next two chapters will show you how to get your business started, attract customers, and build a great reputation.

CHAPTER 2

CREATE YOUR BUSINESS

After you've developed an overarching strategy, it's time to figure out how your customers will find your sharpening service and how to get them to choose your service over your competitors. The marketing and business tactics outlined in this chapter are designed to be low cost, low maintenance, and easy to set up for inexperienced entrepreneurs. My biggest piece of advice is to keep your methods simple for yourself.

Throughout this chapter, I will outline the step-by-step process to get your business off the ground. The steps outlined in this chapter are exactly what I used to get my sharpening service started. It took me a total of two days to set up my business, which could have taken one day if I didn't have to learn and research along the way. I also had a head start because of my familiarity with the industry and my knowledge about building small businesses. It took me a long time to learn all that I did, and by following the steps in this chapter, you can save yourself all that time.

Before publicizing your business, the first step is to purchase your sharpening equipment and learn how to use it. All about that will be covered in the second half of the book. You'll want to have your sharpening equipment in hand and know how to use it before you make your business public so you don't accidentally take an order that you can't fulfill. You'll most likely need to order a lot of your equipment online. The time it takes the equipment to ship to you is a great time to build your website, design your pricing, and so on. Here are the steps to starting your business, in order and in detail.

STEP 1: NAME YOUR BUSINESS

The first step is to pick a name for your sharpening service. I named my sharpening service Next Day Knife Sharpening Santa Fe. I chose this name for several reasons. First, it clearly states what my business does. If the name I chose was something like Kyle's Blade Works, people might look at that name and be confused about what services my business offers. The second and equally important factor to consider when choosing your business name is search engine optimization (SEO). A company called Constant Contact defines SEO as

> ***SEO*** *stands for* ***search engine optimization****. And the phrase "improve your* ***SEO*** *strategy" encompasses the actions taken to ensure your website can be found in a search engine's results page (SERP) when searching for words or phrases relevant to the content on your website.*

SEO is all about figuring out which search terms your customers are likely to use when searching for a business online. When customers search for a sharpening service online, they are most likely going to type the words "sharp," "sharpening," or "knife" into Google or a different search engine. Take a second and think about how you would search for a sharpening service if you wanted your knives sharpened and didn't already know who to contact in your area. I picked Next Day Knife Sharpening Santa Fe as the name for my business because I knew Google would very likely direct people to my web listing if "knife sharpening Santa Fe" was in the name of my business. The two words at the beginning, "next day," are my sales pitch. My sharpening service guarantees that knives will be sharpened and delivered the very next day.

You don't have to follow my naming strategy. There are other ways to increase your SEO without putting the key search terms in your business name. However, in the knife-sharpening world, or for any niche service business, I think it's a good idea to put what you do in your business name. I recommend including either the terms "knife sharpening" or "sharpening service" in your business name.

Once you name your business, you've taken the first major step to making it real. You still have some more work ahead of you, but don't forget to be a little excited. You're about to become a small-business owner, and that's cool.

STEP 2: SET UP A NEW EMAIL ACCOUNT

You'll want to have an email account that's specific to your business, so all your business-related emails don't get mixed in with your personal emails. I highly recommend using Gmail. The comprehensive business tools Google offers for free to those who have Gmail accounts are exceptional. Go to gmail.com and set up a new email address. Use your business name or something related to your business as your email name. Then make sure to use your new email address when creating all your other business-related accounts online.

STEP 3: DESIGN A LOGO

To assist you in building a brand that people recognize, design a logo. I recommend keeping your logo simple and not spending too much time on it. These days, you don't have to pay a graphic designer or an artist a lot of money to design a logo. There are plenty of online resources. My favorite is looka.com. It will cost you about sixty dollars, and after you've designed your logo, you can download it in many different file formats. You can also check to see if the website platform you decide to use has a logo design feature. For instance, Wix is a very popular website platform that offers logo design for no additional cost when you sign up with them.

When considering a logo design, I recommend using fonts and colors that project a sharp and clean feeling, just like people want their knives to be. Logos convey subtle subconscious messages, so it probably wouldn't do a knife-sharpening service any good to have a logo that looks round and dull. I would choose a font with hard corners instead of soft corners, and I wouldn't use too much color. Just keep it clean and simple, and don't spend forever designing it. Once you have a design you like, show it to some family members or friends to get their opinions before you pay to retrieve the files.

STEP 4: CREATE A WEBSITE

My website is one of my two most valuable assets for attracting new business opportunities. The other is my email list, which I'll discuss later. Twenty years ago, building a website took a fair amount of knowledge and skills. These days, they're incredibly easy to build. Anyone with mediocre computer and internet experience can figure it out. You don't need to pay someone to build your website for you. If you aren't great with computers, reach out to a friend or relative who's familiar with computers and ask for help. It's worth it.

CHOOSE A WEBSITE PLATFORM

To build your website, you'll need to pick a website platform. There are many great platforms from which to choose. Any of the good website platforms will offer great tutorials about how to build a website. I chose to use a platform called Wix to build my website, because it was easy to use and low cost. The other two platforms I highly recommend are Squarespace and WordPress.

BUY A DOMAIN

To build a website, you'll need to purchase a website domain, which will become your website's URL. Try to find one that matches your business name or something very close to it. Also, I recommend keeping it short. People don't want to type in ridiculously long website names to find you. When choosing my web domain, I opted not to use nextdayknifesharpeningsantafe.com. That's just too long. So I went with nextdayknife.com—short, sweet, and unique.

There are many places that you can purchase a website domain online. A good place is GoDaddy.com. However, when you decide which website hosting platform you're going to use to build your website, check to see if you can purchase your domain directly from the website hosting platform instead of a third party. Wix, for example, offers domains for sale. If you buy your domain directly from Wix, you won't have to pay to have the domain transferred from the third party to Wix. I wish I had known this when I set up my website, because it would have saved me almost $200. Web domains typically cost between fifteen and sixty dollars. Web domains need to be renewed. You can decide when you purchase yours if you want to buy it for one or two years. If you buy your domain from godaddy.com, run a quick Google search to find a coupon that you can use to save a little money.

START BUILDING YOUR WEBSITE

Once you've chosen a platform, create an account with that platform and start building your website. Keep it simple. Make it easy for people to navigate through your website to find information. These are, in my opinion, the most important components to display on your website:

1. Place an Order—The most important piece of information to display on your website is how customers can place an order with you. It does you no good if the customer reads all about your service, likes what they see, and then can't figure out how to order. This is usually a button that you place in a very easily found location on your website that says something like "place order," "order now," "get a quote," or "schedule a knife pickup." The button redirects either to a page that has your order form or a page that describes how to order.
2. Contact Us—Make your phone number and email address easy to find on your website.
3. How It Works—Walk the customer through the process of exactly what will happen when they place an order with you. This is where you talk about delivery service or provide instructions and directions to drop-off locations or whatever applies in your case. People feel more at ease when ordering from a business for the first time if they know exactly what to expect, and they'll be more likely to order from you if you take the time to explain it.
4. About Us—This is a description of who you are and what makes you different from other sharpening services. Don't overcomplicate your About Us page by telling your whole life story, but make sure to make your description of your business somewhat personal. Keep it simple. Remember: this is about selling yourself and your sharpening service. Talk about the equipment you use and the results you can produce.
5. Pricing—When people are shopping, this is usually the first thing they look for. Make your pricing very easy to find on your website.
6. Testimonials / Reviews—Social proof is incredibly helpful for convincing a new customer to choose you over a different sharpening service. Obviously, you're just getting your business off the ground, and you probably don't have any reviews yet. That's okay. Build this in later, as you start to collect positive reviews. It's very helpful if you can set up your website so your customers can leave reviews themselves, instead of having to email them to you.

PRODUCE OR SOURCE MEDIA CONTENT

Photos and videos go a long way in helping customers to connect with you. These days, many people prefer to watch a video instead of reading an article. I highly recommend shooting a short, thirty-second video about how your sharpening service works and why the customer should choose you. This will make you stand out from the crowd, if it's done right.

You'll need to get some photos to place around your website. Get the highest quality photos that you can, but don't spend too much time or money on this. Most modern smartphones will produce images that will work just fine. If you don't have a camera, you can purchase photos from Adobe Stock at stock.adobe.com or Shutterstock at shutterstock.com. Get some images of knives, your sharpening equipment, of you sharpening a knife, or general photos of people using knives to place around your website. Make sure the images are bright and well-lit and that they clearly demonstrate the message that your business is about knives and sharpening.

CREATE AN ONLINE ORDER FORM

The easiest method I found of creating an order form is to use a Google Form. It's very easy to build, and it's free. The Google Forms feature is one of the reasons I recommended using Gmail for your email address. Once you have a Gmail/Google account, you'll be able to create Google Forms as well as have access to many other resources inside the Google resource center, which is called Google Drive. Simply go to drive.google.com and look for "Forms." This is the information I recommend requesting on your form:

- first and last name
- address
- phone number
- email
- preferred pickup date and time
- preferred delivery date and time
- quantity of knives to sharpen
- a blank box where customers can write in other specific instructions or comments

In addition to requesting information from your customers on the form,

I recommend providing a summary of the ordering process, sharpening process, and your pricing on the top of the form, just in case your customer didn't see it when they were on the main part of your website.

Once you've built and published a Google Form, Google will provide you with a URL that directs to the form. Simply hyperlink the "Place Order" button on your website to this URL, and you're all set.

STEP 5: DESIGN YOUR PRICING STRATEGY

When designing your pricing strategy, there are three important questions to consider:

1. How much money do you believe your time and efforts are worth?
2. How much are people willing to pay to have their knives sharpened?
3. What are your operational costs per knife sharpened?

Start by setting a realistic goal for yourself about how much money you want to make per hour. For me, I decided I wanted to make a bare minimum of thirty dollars an hour for time spent sharpening knives. I divided thirty dollars by the number of knives I could sharpen comfortably in an hour. That number is a minimum of ten knives. So, to make thirty dollars an hour for sharpening, my starting point for my pricing scheme was three dollars per knife.

To answer the question of how much are people willing to pay to have their knives sharpened, you'll need to do a little research. If there are other sharpening services in your area, find out what they are charging per knife. You can also sharpen some knives for family members, friends, or even strangers for free, and then ask them for their honest opinion about how much they would be willing to pay for your service. Collect your data and organize it into a spreadsheet. For instance, if a family member tells you they would pay seven dollars per knife, a friend tells you they would be willing to pay five dollars per knife, and another friend says they would pay three dollars per knife, the average of those would be five dollars per knife. I recommend collecting at least twenty-five samples from a diverse collection of people. This average represents the perceived market value for knife sharpening in your area. Then, weigh that average against the prices that other sharpening services in your area are charging. You'll want to make sure your prices are close to this range.

To figure out your operational cost per knife, you will need to do a bit more math. These are the factors to consider:

- What is the depreciation on your sharpening abrasives?
- What is the total of the monthly payments you make to keep your business running?
- What is your delivery cost, including your time?
- What is the total of the initial investment you made to start your sharpening business divided by the number of months in which you decide you want to make back your initial investment? I recommend twelve months so you can take profits while making back your investment cost.
- What is your monthly marketing/advertising budget?

Here's an example of how to make these calculations. These are based on actual numbers from my sharpening service. If you plan to set up your sharpening service similarly to mine, feel free to use these numbers as your starting point because it will take you a couple of months to collect data. Make sure you do collect data and reevaluate your costs after the first three months.

CALCULATE THE DEPRECIATION ON YOUR SHARPENING ABRASIVES

The second half of this book is where you'll learn all about sharpening equipment and abrasives. For now, we'll use a basic calculation based on the minimum number of abrasives you'll need to sharpen knives professionally. The cost to replace a set of abrasives is $220. The average number of knives that can be sharpened with a set of abrasives before they wear out is approximately 700. Divide $220 by 700 knives and you come out with a depreciation cost of $0.32 per knife sharpened.

CALCULATE YOUR TOTAL MONTHLY EXPENSES

- QuickBooks (accounting software subscription): $26.62
- Wix (website subscription): $6.50
- Constant Contact (email marketing platform subscription): $20
- GoDaddy.com (website domain renewal): $12 per year equals $1 per month
- Office Supplies (average per month): $10

Total: $64.12

Divide this number by the minimum number of knives you think you'll sharpen in an average month. I believed I would sharpen absolutely no less than 100 knives per month. So, $64.12 in total monthly expenses divided by 100 knives rounds to $0.64 per knife.

CALCULATE YOUR DELIVERY COSTS (IF APPLICABLE TO YOUR BUSINESS MODEL)

To calculate this, try to figure out how much time it will take and the total distance you'll travel to make one pickup and one delivery, round trip. Remember: if you're running a pickup and delivery service, you'll make one round trip to pick up knives and another round trip to drop them off. So multiply your round-trip cost by two. Sometimes, you'll have days on which you only deliver to one customer. Your cost decreases as you add more stops to your route, but it's good practice to calculate costs based on highest possible costs. That way, when you reduce costs, the difference becomes profits in your pocket. Based on the area that I live in and traffic conditions, I calculated the average round trip would take ten minutes to travel an average of two miles. You then have to consider how many knives your average customer will have sharpened at a time. For me, that number is five. With that information, you can make calculations:

Labor Cost per Delivery: Hourly rate you want to be paid (as decided above) equals thirty dollars per hour. Thirty dollars per hour equals $0.50 per minute. Ten-minute round trip equals five dollars per trip.

Mileage Cost per Delivery: The federal mileage reimbursement rate is $0.575 per mile, as of 2020. Instead of trying to calculate your gas mileage and vehicle wear and tear yourself, just use that to calculate your mileage cost. For a two-mile round trip, your cost would be $1.15.

Now, take your labor cost per trip ($5), add it to your vehicle cost per trip ($1.15), and multiply by two because you'll be making a second round-trip for delivery. The total comes to $12.30. Now, divide that by the average number of knives sharpened by each customer; $12.30 divided by five equals $2.46. That's your average delivery cost per knife based on the highest cost scenario of making only one pickup or delivery each time you run a route. That sounds like a lot, but remember, it's calculated in that you'll be paying yourself $30 per hour for your driving time.

CALCULATE YOUR INITIAL INVESTMENT COSTS

To calculate this, add up all the money you spent to get your business off the ground. This includes your initial purchases for your equipment, your costs to build drop boxes, your one-time setup payments for online services, and so on. Mine looked like this:

- Sharpening Equipment: $554.00
- Other sharpening supplies: $84.87
- Logo: $60.00
- Office supplies: $43.32
- Business cards: $31.50
- Web domain: $50.12
- Web domain transfer: $180.00

Total: $1,003.81

If you want to make back your initial investment within the first twelve months (on top of paying yourself and covering your other expenses), divide your total start-up cost by twelve. This comes to $83.65 per month for my initial investment. Then divide that number by the minimum number of knives you think you'll sharpen in a month (already decided above). If that number is 100, divide $83.65 by 100, which equals $0.84 per knife.

CALCULATE YOUR MONTHLY ADVERTISING BUDGET

How to advertise your business will be covered in detail in the next chapter. For now, pick an estimate of how much you would like to spend per month in advertising to attract new customers. When it comes to advertising, the more you put in, the more you'll get out, as long as you are concentrating your efforts in strategies you've proven to generate returns. My monthly advertising budget for my sharpening service when I first got started was $100. Divide that by the minimum number of knives you think you'll sharpen in a month (100), and you get one dollar per knife.

CALCULATE YOUR TOTAL COST PER KNIFE

Add up your per-knife costs from each of the above categories.

- Equipment depreciation: $0.32 per knife
- Monthly expenses: $0.64 per knife
- Delivery cost: $2.46 per knife
- Initial investment cost: $0.84 per knife
- Marketing/advertising cost: $1.00 per knife

Total Cost: $5.26

Add that to the amount you would like to be paid for your labor. For me, that's $3 per knife. So, add $3 to $5.26, and the total price per knife comes to $8.26. I recommend rounding this to the nearest dollar or half dollar, to make things easier on you and your customers.

Now that you have a good starting number, compare that to the research you've done about what other sharpening services are charging and how much you estimate people will pay to have their knives sharpened. If your price comes in lower than the perceived market value for knife sharpening, that's great. You can be super competitive with your pricing, or you have some room to increase your prices and generate more income. If your pricing comes in above the perceived market value for knife sharpening, you'll have to make some decisions about how to move forward.

I found that the right price point for knife sharpening in Santa Fe was between $5.00 and $8.00 per knife. I started off with lower prices to build my sharpening service and develop a reputation, and I gradually increased my prices over time once my business was established. In early 2021, I raised my prices to $8.00 per knife, and my customers did not complain because I had developed a great reputation and accumulated a significant number of positive reviews.

Generally, I have seen higher prices for knife sharpening in metropolitan areas and lower prices in rural areas. The perceived market value for knife sharpening in San Francisco, for instance, may be as high as $15.00 per knife. The perceived market value for sharpening in a Midwest town of 2,000 people may be as low as $3.00 per knife. This has to do with costs of living and other variables. You may decide to choose a lower or higher base rate, depending on where you live and your lifestyle.

A different pricing strategy that I have seen commonly used in the sharpening service industry is pricing by blade length. For instance, a service may charge one dollar per blade inch. This would come out to $8.00 for an eight-inch chef's knife, and $4.00 for a four-inch pocketknife. Under the assumption that larger knives take longer to sharpen, I see how this makes sense. That said, I don't recommend this strategy. If a customer wants to figure out how much it will cost them to sharpen their set of kitchen knives, they probably don't want to have to get their tape measure out and calculate it themselves. It will also take you time to measure all the knives you sharpen and then calculate prices. Not to mention, in my experience and with the sharpening techniques I'm going to tell you about later in this book, the difference in time to sharpen a larger knife compared to a smaller knife is nominal. I recommend keeping it simple and sticking to a flat rate per knife.

As your sharpening business grows, you'll find ways to reduce costs. For instance, a few of these may include:

- After your first year, you'll have paid off your initial investment, which will automatically provide you with a significant per-knife cost reduction.
- If you offer pickup and delivery services on a few specific days of the week, compared to every day, you'll accumulate more stops on each route, which will reduce your per-knife delivery cost.
- Once you've established your business and collected a sizable contact list, you can reduce how much money you spend on marketing.

I recommend doing a cost assessment at least twice a year so you can have an idea about where you stand. It's good practice in any business to check in on your costs periodically. Always be on the lookout for cost reductions, but never reduce costs to the point where the quality of the service you provide suffers.

MULTITIERED PRICING

Some knife-sharpening services offer multiple tiers of pricing for different qualities of results. For instance, to create a very shiny, sharper edge on a high-end knife that belongs to a knife collector, you'll need to spend more time and use additional equipment to sharpen that knife. If you offer a service that meets that type of demand, and you also sharpen for people who don't care how shiny their edge is, you may consider adding pricing tiers into your sharpening service's pricing model. For instance, some sharpening services offer one price for basic sharpening, and another price for "expert" sharpening to produce a more refined and sharper edge. If you decide to offer different pricing tiers, remember to go back to your cost equation and make adjustments to your initial investment cost for your sharpening equipment, your depreciation on equipment cost, and your labor-per-knife cost to calculate your costs and pricing for each tier.

Though offering multiple pricing tiers is worth considering, specifically because you can use the different levels of sharpness to upsell your customers to spend more with you, I actually don't recommend multitiered pricing for most part-time sharpening services. This is because I strongly believe in the value of keeping things easy to understand for customers. When I tried to offer multiple levels of pricing, I received a lot of questions from my customers about what the difference was in sharpness and if they really needed to pay the higher-level price. Sometimes, customers felt disappointed because they wanted the higher level of sharpening but didn't want to pay for it. After I switched to a one-price model, customers felt like they were receiving the best I could offer without getting caught up in the details and asking themselves what more I could have done for them. Multitiered pricing was not the right solution for my sharpening service because I focus my service primarily on one customer group, but that doesn't mean it can't be a good solution for other sharpening services. If you decided to target your sharpening service toward two very different customer groups (general household customers and collectors of high-end knives) multitiered pricing may be a good choice for you.

DELIVERY FEE

If you choose to start a pickup and delivery sharpening business, you may wish to consider charging a delivery fee. If you find yourself in the car more than you expected, or if you're spending more on gas than you want to, you can add a delivery fee. However, in my experience delivery fees can be a turnoff for some customers. If one sharpening service charges twenty-five dollars to sharpen five knives and offers free delivery, and another sharpening service charges twenty dollars for five knives plus a five-dollar delivery fee, it's my experience that customers will more often choose the service that is not charging the fee. Even though the total price comes to the same amount in either scenario, psychologically, people don't react well to the word *fee*, whereas they love the word *free*. What I have found to be successful is increasing my pricing per knife to cover my delivery cost and setting a zone in which I offer free delivery. My zone is the city limits, and I charge a five-dollar delivery fee to customers who live outside the city limits. If customers are in an extremely inconvenient location, I will increase my delivery fee on a case-by-case basis. Or I sometimes ask the customer if they can meet me the next time they're in town.

To summarize, these are the steps to take to get your website up and running:

1. Choose a website platform – Wix, Squarespace, and Wordpress are all good choices
2. Purchase a domain – godaddy.com is a great place to shop for a domain. Don't forget to find a coupon on Google before you checkout!
3. Create your content
4. Write the content for your "About Us" page
5. Write the content for your "How it Works" page
6. Source images that you can use for your home page and other places around your website
7. Calculate your costs and set your pricing
8. Design and build your website using all the content and media that you've already produced or gathered
9. Build your online order form (if applicable to your business model) – I recommend using a Google Form

STEP 6: PUBLISH YOUR WEBSITE

Remember: don't do this until you have your sharpening equipment in hand and know how to use it. Once you do, publish your website and then take a little time to celebrate. You can now consider yourself a small-business owner. It was at this point for me that I felt a wave of accomplishment and excitement rush over me, and it changed my life forever.

STEP 7: SET UP A GOOGLE BUSINESS LISTING

This is incredibly important, as most customers will find your website by searching on Google. If your business isn't registered with Google, customers will have a much harder time finding you. Registering with Google is completely free, so there's no reason to not do it.

Go to Google and search for "Google My Business." Make sure you're already signed in to Google with the Gmail account you already created for your business. When you arrive at the Google My Business page, create a business account. The process is easy to follow. These are the most important pieces of information you'll need to input into Google:

- your business name
- your phone number
- your website address
- description of your business and the services you offer
- photos that include knives

STEP 8: SET UP A YELP BUSINESS LISTING

Next to Google, Yelp is the next most common platform that people use to search for businesses and services. Registering with Yelp is also free. Go to biz.yelp.com and click "Manage My Free Listing." Setting up your business with Yelp is also quite easy. Remember to use your business's email address when registering. When prompted, input the same information that you put in your Google listing:

- your business name
- your phone number
- your website address
- description of your business and the services you offer
- photos that include knives

STEP 9: SET UP PAYMENT METHODS

The last essential piece to setting up your business is deciding how you'll accept payment for your services. My recommendation is to make it easy for your customers to pay you. To make it easy for your customers, it's best if you accept many different forms of payment. Some people will prefer to pay with cash, and others will prefer to pay via credit card or PayPal. It would be a difficult situation to deliver knives to a customer who didn't have cash available, and you didn't have a way to accept credit cards or other forms of electronic payment.

Whichever payment methods you choose to accept, make sure your acceptable methods of payment are visible on your website and on your order form so your customers can be prepared.

Set up a new bank account for your business. This isn't required, but I highly recommend it so you can keep your personal and business finances separate. If you're going to accept electronic payments, link those services to your business bank account. Make sure your name and your business name are both registered on the account. This is easy to set up, and only takes about an hour. Go to a bank branch of your choosing and tell them you would like to set up a new business checking account. To do this, you will need a federal tax ID number or Employer Identification Number (EIN). How to obtain this will be covered in chapter 5.

CASH

Accepting cash payments is the easiest. Always keep a minimum of twenty to forty dollars in small bills and change with you when you are delivering knives.

CREDIT CARDS

To accept credit cards, you'll need to register with a credit card processing company. I highly recommend Square Point of Sale. Download the Square Point of Sale app on your smartphone or go to squareup.com and follow the steps to register your account. It takes about five minutes. They'll send you a credit card reader that attaches directly to your smartphone for free! When accepting credit cards as a form of payment, know that you'll have to pay a percentage of each transaction to the credit card processing company. Transaction fees are usually about 3 percent. Currently (2020), Square charges 2.6 percent plus $0.10 for every transaction.

OTHER ELECTRONIC PAYMENT METHODS

Generally, you probably won't need to accept payment electronically other than via credit card. However, it doesn't hurt to have a PayPal account, just in case. Setting up a PayPal account is easy. Just go to PayPal.com, click "Sign Up" and follow the step-by-step process to set up your account.

Then link your business's bank account to your PayPal account. I've also had a few customers ask if they can pay me with Venmo. It doesn't hurt to offer this as a payment method, as it's free to you. Go to the app store on your smartphone and download the Venmo app and link your business's bank account to it. It takes about five to ten minutes to set up.

INVOICING

If you have business customers, you'll need to have a method of generating invoices. QuickBooks Online is an easy platform to use to generate invoices and keep track of which invoices have been paid and which are still outstanding.

CHECKLIST

Here's a checklist you can use to complete the steps discussed in this chapter. It also includes the estimated cost for each step.

Action	Notes/Resource Link	Cost Estimate	Complete?
Name your business	Choose a name that includes "knife sharpening" or "sharpening service"	Free	
Set up a business email address with Gmail	gmail.com	Free	
Design a logo	Looka.com or Wix	$60	
Purchase a website domain name	Godaddy.com, or buy a domain from the website platform you choose to build your website	$20 to $55	
Pick a website platform and build out your website	Wix.com Squarespace.com wordpress.com	$12 to $40, billed monthly	
Produce or source media content for your website	iMovie app for iPhone stock.adobe.com shutterstock.com	Free	
Build an order form	drive.google.com	Free	
Design your pricing	Set target income, calculate costs, compare to perceived market value	Free	
Publish your website	Hold off on doing this until you have your sharpening equipment and you know how to use it	No additional cost	
Set up a Google business listing	Google My Business	Free	
Set up a Yelp business listing	biz.yelp.com	Free	
Set up a business checking account	Local or national bank. Remember to get a Federal Tax ID Number or EIN first	Free	
Set up payment methods	Square Point of Sale app, Paypal.com, Venmo app	No upfront cost	

Total approximate cost to start website, online business listings, and payment methods: $92 to $155.

After you've completed the steps in this chapter, customers will be able to find you, and you'll be able to accept their business. Customers being able to find you and your being able to accept their business are two big components of getting your business off the ground. The marketing and advertising methods described in the next chapter are about how you can find new customers and convince them to give you their business.

CHAPTER 3

ADVERTISING AND MARKETING

Once your business is off the ground, it's time to start finding customers. When you first get started, I recommend being aggressive in your efforts to attract new customers. As the owner of a sharpening service, your job in marketing isn't to find people who have knives, because everyone has knives and everyone is a potential customer. Instead, your job is going to be to convince people to have their knives sharpened and then to hold onto your customers after they have done business with you.

Many people understand the value of sharp knives and appreciate having their knives sharpened. I consider these people low-hanging fruit. These are the people who will seek you out. They'll find your website, contact you, and place orders. However, many people don't have a very strong appreciation for sharp knives. They simply don't know how satisfying it is to cut through something with an incredibly sharp knife, so they don't understand the value in having their knives sharpened by a professional with top-of-the-line equipment. They know knives need to be sharpened because they've been taught that about knives, but they often don't connect that knowledge with an emotion like satisfaction or joy. It should be your number one job in marketing your sharpening service to show people how they will *feel* when they cut something with a knife you've sharpened. If you can do that, you'll succeed in this business.

The strategies outlined in this chapter worked for me. After a short amount of time, I was able to build a sizable customer list that I could then market to throughout the year. The marketing tactics in this chapter are designed to be low cost and low maintenance, designed primarily for people who have never started a business before.

The largest market segment for knife sharpening is household kitchen knives. I suggest you build your business around that. However, there are exceptions to this tactic. For instance, if you know a lot of hunters or you're in the military, you may wish to focus your sharpening service to the people you know and focus less on household knives. But for most of you, the household market should be your bread and butter. So how will you make these households aware of your service, and then convince them to use your service once they're aware of your business? Read on.

FACEBOOK AND INSTAGRAM

Create Facebook and Instagram pages for your business. Populate them with the same content you used for your website. Creating a business page on both platforms is free, but you need to link them to a personal account to manage them. If you're not already on Facebook or Instagram with a personal account, create a personal account on both platforms. Once you have a personal account, you can create a separate page for your business. In my opinion, Facebook and Instagram are the most valuable social media platforms for a small service-type business to establish a presence. It won't cost you anything to set up a business page on either Facebook or Instagram.

Once your business profiles are created, invite your entire friends list to like your business pages. Ask your friends for help to spread the word about your business. It's easy. Just create a post with an image of you sharpening a knife and say something along the lines of this:

> *Hey, everyone! I just started a new business sharpening knives! I would love it if you would like my page and share it to anyone you know who you think might appreciate having their knives sharpened. I'm excited to be doing this, and I would love to have all your help to get this off the ground!*

Once your Facebook page starts gaining likes, and it will, start posting content a couple times a week to keep your service fresh on people's minds. I've found these types of posts to be successful:

- images of you sharpening knives
- images of knives

- images and videos of knives being used and cutting through things very easily
- announcements of community events you'll be sponsoring or attending
- images or videos of you delivering knives to happy customers
- announcements of any promotions you might be running
- positive testimonials from your customers

If you want to reach more people more quickly, you can consider boosting your posts. To do this, you'll need to pay a small amount of money and the social platform will put your post in front of more people than just the people who follow your page. For just ten to twenty dollars, you can reach a few hundred or even a few thousand people.

Always caption your images and videos and create posts with the goal of sparking an emotional response. Choose your own strategy about how to talk to and present information to your customers. Be unique. I've found that I get better responses when I trigger a positive emotional response compared to a negative emotional response. For instance, instead of posting things like "It sucks to use dull knives," I say things like "It's super satisfying to use sharp knives." I've found I get the most engagements with posts when I include a short video of a knife doing something only a very sharp knife can do, like cutting paper-thin tomato slices, and captioning the video with something like this: "Can your knives do this?"

When posting on Facebook or any other social media platform, I recommend posting information that's useful to your customers. If people only see you trying to get attention, they won't want to follow you. Instead, mix up your posts by providing useful information and content that provides value to your audience. These are some ideas you can use:

- How to care for your knives so they won't become dull so fast
- Wood cutting board vs. resin cutting board—which one is better for your knives?
- Do you know the suggested use for a chef's knife vs. a carving knife?
- Proper way to hold your knives
- Safety tips for knife use and storage

You don't have to create all the content for these posts yourself. Though it's important to create your own content so you don't seem unauthentic, you can also borrow content from other people. Thousands of YouTube videos exist out there about knife use and maintenance. Feel free to link to them in your Facebook posts. The content creators will be thankful because you're sending them more traffic, and you can save yourself a lot of time by not having to produce your own content. When you borrow content, make sure you give credit to the original content producer and link back to where the original content was posted.

Your strategy on Facebook and Instagram should be to gain as many followers as you can, within your area of business. The more people who follow you, the more people you can market your services to for free. To gain followers, I find it helpful to engage with your audience by offering giveaways and contests. Like-and-share campaigns are a very common way to gain followers on social media. A sharpening service's giveaway campaign would look something like this: Make a post with an image that's relevant to your business, and caption it with "I'm giving free sharpening to three lucky people this week. Like my page and share this post to enter for your chance to win!" Then pick three winners at random from the people who liked and shared your post and contact them to tell them they've won. Find out how you can pick up their knives, and then sharpen them. In addition to gaining followers, you'll get to show three people what you can do by sharpening their knives. If you do an excellent job, those people will likely contact you next time they need their knives sharpened and recommend you to their friends.

NEXT DOOR

Nextdoor.com is a wonderful community-based social media platform. If you don't know about Next Door, I highly recommend getting acquainted with it. This platform offers you the opportunity to make your sharpening service known to your direct community. You can post as a community member or as a business. Just like Facebook and Instagram, you'll need to create a personal account before you can create a business account.

Next Door won't let you post about your business for free. But there are ways around that. If you create a post to simply tell people that you just started a sharpening service in the area, and let them know they can send you a message for details, Next Door won't flag your post as a business post. As soon as you include a website link or any pricing information in your post, Next Door's algorithm will flag your post as business-related and prevent you from publishing it. If you do want to advertise as a business, that option is available and low cost.

The strategy I use on Next Door is that of being a friendly neighbor with a small business. I periodically remind people that my service exists, announce promotions, and announce community events. I don't recommend posting more than six times per year on Next Door.

BUSINESS CARDS

Design a business card and get it printed. I recommend putting a picture or a sketch of a knife on your card so people remember who you are. Without a business card, you'll miss a lot of opportunities. You may meet dozens of people who are interested in your service, but they will not know how to contact you if you don't hand them a business card. Handing out business cards to everyone who seems interested in your service and giving a couple of business cards to everyone who hires you to sharpen their knives will rapidly increase your business's organic growth rate.

I use vistaprint.com to design and print business cards. They have great, user-friendly design tools so you don't have to hire someone else to design your card. They are affordable, fast, and produce nice-quality cards.

When you deliver knives to customers, always leave a few business cards with the knives. This way, if customers want to recommend you to a friend, they can simply give your card to their friend.

Magnetic business cards that people can use as refrigerator magnets are significantly more expensive, but they're a great marketing tool. People love to receive things they can use. If your card is up on their refrigerator, they'll see it every day and likely place a new order with you sooner. If you're going to design magnetic cards, make sure they look good. People won't use them if they aren't visually appealing. You can order magnetic cards from vistaprint.com.

SHARPENING IN PUBLIC

One of the best methods I have found to attract new customers is to set up my sharpener in a public place and sharpen knives. If you do this, people will become interested and be curious about what you're doing.

They'll approach you, and then you can tell them all about your sharpening service. Make sure to check with the property manager before you set up your sharpener and start sharpening knives. Even if you set up a sharpener in a public park, check with your city's parks department to make sure it's okay.

When sharpening knives in public, make sure to bring plenty of knives to work on. This is a great opportunity to practice and hone your skills. If you don't have knives from customers to sharpen that day, bring some of your own knives or sharpen some knives for friends and family members. Some people walking by may have pocketknives with them, and you can offer to sharpen those. If your goal is to meet new potential customers and build relationships, I recommend sharpening at least the first knife for someone for free and collecting contact information instead of currency. If someone brings you more than one knife to sharpen, I think it's safe to charge for your sharpening services. Bring business cards and an email sign-up sheet with you, plus some pens and a notepad.

SHARPNESS DEMONSTRATIONS

An excellent way to engage with your customers and to inspire them to have an emotional reaction is to let them feel firsthand what it's like to cut through something with a knife you have sharpened. Let them feel the satisfaction of cutting with an incredibly sharp knife. Whenever you can, set up your sharpener in a place people will be, and give live demonstrations. Bring some tomatoes with you and let the people who approach you cut through them. They'll be impressed, and they'll want to do business with you because they'll want their knives at home to perform like the knife they just used. Make sure to give everyone a business card, because even if they don't place an order with you right then and there, they'll likely order after the next time they use their dull knives at home. When you perform sharpness demonstrations and let your customer handle the knives, make sure to give your customers cut-proof gloves to wear when they handle the knives to avoid accidents and liabilities.

HOST COMMUNITY EVENTS

People love to support new local businesses, and they especially love to support local businesses who give back to their community. Hosting a public event, like a community barbecue at a public park, is a great method to attract new customers and start off on the right foot with them. It will cost you some money, but it will pay for itself and a lot more with the new business you'll attract. It's also fun. Who doesn't enjoy a good barbecue?

If you're going to host a community event, you'll need to advertise it. Nextdoor.com is a great place to do this. You can also try putting up flyers or signs, taking out an ad in a local paper, or spreading the word via social media. To be successful in getting the word out, I recommend using a combination of these advertising strategies.

How do you get people to come to a community event? Offer something for free. Free food always attracts people. You can also offer free knife sharpening, but possibly limit it to one to two knives per person. If you're going to offer free food and offer free knife sharpening, you'll need help. Bring a friend along to do the grilling while you sharpen knives. You don't have to be sharpening the whole time, and I recommend against that. Get out and mingle with people— tell them about what you do and find out about them as well.

You can ask other local businesses if they would like to co-sponsor the event with you. Find some businesses that you like and get in touch with the person who handles their marketing. Be prepared to talk about locations, times, advertising strategies, and how each business will contribute to the logistics. Co-sponsoring provides the benefit of shared responsibilities, so all the legwork doesn't all fall on you. An established local business will also likely have an existing customer following and a means of contacting them, so your turnout will likely be better than if you organize and host the event by yourself.

While at the event, be prepared to take contact information from your customers. If people express interest in having their knives sharpened by you, take their information. If you hand out a business card, their interest may dissipate later, so it's best that you have their information so you can follow up with them instead of waiting for them to follow up with you.

Hosting a community event is the most expensive marketing strategy discussed in this chapter, but it's also the most effective. The money you spend will more than pay for itself if you take the time to do it right, get to know the people in your community, make your business known, and collect contact information so you can follow up with people later.

NEWSPAPER ADS

Taking out newspaper ads is inexpensive and may be a good way for you to attract new customers, especially when you're first starting off. Contact your local newspaper or go on their website and learn about how to take an ad out, the pricing, and the word or area limit for each pricing tier. All you need to do is give a brief, one-to-two-sentence overview of your business and provide the name of your website. I recommend running an ad for seven to fourteen consecutive days.

EMAIL MARKETING

I can't state strongly enough how crucial it is to build an email list. When it comes to marketing, my email list and my website are my two most valuable assets. The power of email marketing is incredible. It works well for a knife-sharpening business because people often need a little reminder to have their knives sharpened. That being said, people will get very annoyed with you if you send them too many emails. I have found that the right number of emails to send is about four to six per customer, per year, plus occasional announcements of promotions and events. I would not send a marketing email more than once a month. People get too many emails these days, and if they get more emails than once a month from you, they will be a lot more likely to unsubscribe from your email list.

Try to collect an email address from every customer who orders with you or who seems interested in your service. You may try offering an incentive to collect email addresses. For instance, if you set up a table at a farmers market, you may try offering one knife sharpened for free if the customer provides you with their email address.

There are privacy laws in America about email marketing, so you must be careful. This is one of the main reasons it's best to set up an account with an email marketing platform like Constant Contact or Klaviyo. When you send a marketing email, you need to include a privacy policy, your address, and an unsubscribe link in the email footer; there are other regulations as well. Email marketing platforms take care of this for you, so you don't have to worry about formatting your emails correctly or writing your own privacy policy.

Email marketing platforms also allow you to create more professional-looking emails than you could from your Gmail account. You can add nice imagery, choose fonts, use background colors or images, and many more features. You can build custom email lists to sort your customers into categories. With an email marketing platform, you can collect data about how your customers interacted with your emails, like how many people opened the email and how many of those people clicked a link. Using an email marketing platform will also save you a ton of time because you won't have to send emails to customers one by one.

If you're operating your sharpening service as a side business, and your goal is to earn $10,000 per year in revenue, you should aim to build an email list over time of at least 500 contacts consisting of people who you've sharpened knives for at least once. Once you establish an email list this size, you can start to scale back your aggressive marketing efforts to attract new customers because you'll likely be able to earn a significant portion of your revenue goal from your existing customer base, provided your customers had an enjoyable experience when they conducted business with you the first time. That's not to say you should cease all your other outward marketing efforts, but with a solid email list of happy customers, you won't have to do so much work to earn business.

REVIEWS AND TESTIMONIALS

How many times have you seen a pop-up on a website or an app or received an email from a company asking you for a review? Any company that's good at marketing asks their customers for reviews regularly, and they do this because reviews and testimonials work. Having good reviews and testimonials can be the deciding factor that gets someone to choose your sharpening service over one of your competitors or a knife-sharpening product. In my experience, reviews and testimonials don't come in very frequently unless you ask your customers for them. The best time to ask a customer for a review is shortly after you've delivered their knives.

There are many platforms where customers can leave reviews. For service-type business, the most common places people leave/find reviews are on Google, Yelp, Facebook, and the company's website. Devise a way of asking your customers to leave reviews, such as a follow-up email after you complete the transaction that links to the pages where you would like them to leave a review about your sharpening service. You could also print up a note to deliver to each customer when you return their knives, thanking them for their business and providing instructions about how to leave you a review.

When soliciting reviews, you should want to receive reviews from happy customers. It doesn't do you any good to ask a disappointed customer to leave you a review. Most big companies use what's called a net promoter score (NPS) survey to find out if a customer is happy and going to leave a good review, or an unhappy customer who's going to leave a bad review. I'm sure you've seen this before. It's one simple question: "How likely are you to recommend (insert business name) to a friend?" The response is a one to ten scale, with one being not likely to recommend, and ten being very likely to recommend. When a customer responds with an eight or above, the company will immediately ask the customer to leave a review. If the customer responds with a seven or lower, the company will usually send the customer an email asking for information about how they think the company could improve.

As a small service, setting up an NPS survey is probably not necessary. You have the opportunity to engage with your customers face-to-face so you can gauge their feelings about your service in real life. As a small, community-based service, I implore you to always try to go above and beyond when it comes to customer service. Did you make sure to test the knives for sharpness before you delivered them to the customer? Were you on time? Was the experience easy and convenient for the customer? Did you proactively communicate with your customer? Always take the time to ask yourself with each customer if you're providing the best service that you can. If you always answer that question with yes, you'll likely have happy customers who leave good reviews.

If you do come across an unhappy customer, take the time to ask them why they weren't satisfied with your service, so you can learn and improve. Also, try to change their opinion by offering a compensation like a coupon for free sharpening, resharpening their knives if they weren't pleased with the results, or simply refunding their money. Try to always do the right thing when it comes to your customers. Put yourself in their shoes. If you paid for a service and were unsatisfied with the results, what would you expect from the company to make it right?

EMAIL CONFIRMATIONS

Email confirmations are a great way of gaining trust with your customers. These days, people expect to receive an email confirmation after they place an order. If you don't confirm their order via email, your customer service reputation may suffer. Order confirmation emails should be short and sweet. This is what mine looks like:

> *Hi (insert customer's first name),*
>
> *Thank you for choosing (insert your business name) and for your order! Your knife pickup is scheduled for (insert date and time). I will give you a call shortly prior to your pickup time to confirm I'm on the way.*
>
> *I will have your knives sharpened and delivered back to you on (insert delivery time and date). Payment is due at the time of delivery. Your estimated total will be (insert estimated total). I accept cash, check, and all major credit cards.*
>
> *If you have any questions or need to change your pickup and delivery times, please give me a call at (insert phone number) or reply to this email.*
>
> *Thank you! I hope you have a wonderful day!*

After you deliver knives, send the customer a follow-up email. This second email is a great opportunity to provide useful information to the customer and to solicit a review. In business, I have always found that it's best to give the customer something before you ask them for something. In this case, I give some tips about knife care, and then I ask for the review. This is what my follow-up email looks like:

> *Thank you for choosing (insert your business name). Your knives were delivered on (insert delivery date). They are* very *sharp. Please handle them with care. If you notice anything unsatisfactory about your knives, their performance, or if you have any questions, please don't hesitate to contact me.*
>
> *These are some tips you can use to keep your knives in great shape:*
>
> - *Dishwashing machines are the number one killer of knife edges. To keep your knives sharp, I recommend always washing them by hand.*
> - *Never leave your knives under water in your sink. Not only is this dangerous because you can't see them, but also, it's bad for your edges.*

- *Always use a cutting board. Wood cutting boards are better for your knives than resin or plastic cutting boards.*
- *Try to avoid storing your knives in a drawer where they can bang around and into each other. Knife blocks are a better solution, and magnetic knife racks are even better.*

I would greatly appreciate it if you would be willing to take a few minutes and leave me a review. My business is growing, and I can use all the help I can get! There are several places where you can leave a review about my sharpening service:

- *Yelp (insert link to Yelp page)*
- *Google (insert link to Google page)*
- *Facebook (insert link to your Facebook page)*

If you don't have accounts with any of these services, you can email me your review, and I'll put it up on my website. Again, I'm very grateful for your time to do this. Thank you.

When you're ready to schedule your next sharpening, please visit (insert your website URL). You may also give me a call at (insert phone number) or send me an email at (insert email address).

It was a pleasure doing business with you. I hope you enjoy using your knives!

This email is a little lengthy, but it has proven to be successful time and time again. My customers love receiving the tips about knife care, and a surprising amount of them take the time to leave a review. In my experience, people love to support small businesses, and sometimes, you just need to ask for their support and tell them how they can help you.

PROMOTIONS

Offering promotions is another strategy you can use to drive in more business. The promotion I usually offer is five knives for twenty dollars. During the winter holidays and while this promotion is active, it's not uncommon for me to sharpen knives for five households per day, which equates to $100 or more in revenue per day.

The other type of promotion I've had success with is a first-time-customer promotion. For a customer's first order with me, I will offer one or two knives for free, regardless of the number of knives they give me to sharpen.

This type of promotion is a great tool for attracting new customers and building relationships.

In early 2020, I moved to a different part of town, and as a result, my business's volume fell off fairly substantially. When the 2020 COVID-19 pandemic hit, I decided to offer a community giveback—two free knives sharpened to anyone, with no minimum number of knives sharpened to qualify for the promotion. During the pandemic, people cooked most of their meals at home, and I thought it would be nice to give them the little comfort of using sharp knives to cook with, and I also wanted to use this opportunity to jump-start my business in the new part of town. I made one post to my new neighborhood area on Nextdoor.com to advertise the promotion. The campaign was a success. Over a ten-day period, I sharpened knives for twenty-six new customers. I sharpened 142 knives for a total of $462 in revenue, plus $115 in tips. Only three customers gave me two knives to sharpen, and on average customers gave me four or more knives to sharpen. I gave all my customers several business cards which they could give to people they know, and I sent a follow-up email to each customer asking for a review. As a result of the campaign, my new customers began to refer me to their friends and neighbors, I received five very positive reviews, and directly following the campaign my business's revenue was back up to where it was before I moved.

Though promotions are a great way to drive in business temporarily and find new customers, they can come back to bite you if you run too many promotions. In my experience, most people don't want or need to have their knives sharpened more than two to four times per year. If people get used to seeing your promotions, they will wait to have their knives sharpened until you offer your next promotion. If you offer too many promotions, you'll see your business come in waves surrounding your promotions instead of a steady stream of business and cash flow throughout the year. I recommend running no more than two price-reduction promotions and no more than two to three new-customer promotions per year.

There are other incentive-based promotions you can offer that don't involve discounting your pricing. Feel free to get creative and have fun with your promotions. For example, you could run a promotion like this: *This week only, get a free pineapple when you have five or more knives sharpened*! Then give a juicy, over-the-top description of the pineapple and show some great images of it, specifically of the pineapple being cut by a newly sharpened knife.

Someone out there could see your advertisement, laugh, and say to him- or herself, *You know, I don't know if my knives need to be sharpened that badly, but man, I really want that pineapple!*

BULK-PRICING DEALS

When operating a knife-sharpening service, it's important to try to maximize the number of knives you sharpen per customer. To do this, I recommend offering a bulk-pricing deal. For instance, my normal price per knife is $8.00. But I also offer a year-round special, which reduces the price to $7.00 per knife when the customer has five or more knives sharpened at a time. I've found that most people can find at least five knives lying around their house to be sharpened. To give you an idea of the number of people who take advantage of this offer, over 80 percent of my customers have five or more knives sharpened each time they do business with me. This is why I say you only need to find ten customers per week to hit a profit goal of $250 per week. Maximizing the number of knives you sharpen per customer is crucial for success in this business.

FLYERS

Make some nice-looking flyers and put them up around town. Grocery stores and coffee shops usually have bulletin boards, as do shopping centers. Make sure to include the following information on your flyers:

- your logo
- your business name
- "knife sharpening"
- your phone number
- your website
- your pricing (optional—some people leave pricing off flyers to give customers a reason to call or visit a website)
- a brief sales pitch about your sharpening service and how it works
- in image to catch people's attention

DOOR-TO-DOOR

Going door-to-door to sell your sharpening service may seem very 1950s, but it does actually work. Because knife sharpening is relatively inexpensive, and every household has knives, knocking on doors and handing out business cards or flyers is a great way to meet new potential customers. If you decided to use this strategy to promote your business, focus your efforts in neighborhoods where you are more likely to be successful. I have been most successful in middle-class and upper-class neighborhoods, where there are concentrations of people in their fifties and older. In my experience, younger people are more apprehensive about strangers showing up at their doors. Make sure to be dressed professionally and be extraordinarily friendly. Some people will likely give you their knives to sharpen right then and there, so make sure you have order forms and a few knife bins to collect knives with you.

It's generally a terrible idea to approach people's houses with a knife in your hand. If you plan to give a sharpness demonstration, which isn't a bad idea, you can avoid getting shot by keeping the knife in your bag until you tell the customer you would like to perform a demonstration. Pull out your cutting board first, then the tomatoes or whatever you're going to use for your demonstration, and then pull out the knife.

KNIFE-SHARPENING SEASONALITY

Like most businesses, knife-sharpening services experience seasonality. There are busier times of the year, and there are slower times of the year. It's important to know about these times so you can plan your marketing efforts accordingly.

- November and December—This is the busiest time of the year, by far. The two biggest cooking holidays, Thanksgiving and Christmas, are the most important holidays for a knife-sharpening service to capitalize on.
- March—Easter is the third largest cooking holiday of the year, and I've had success with promotions around this time.
- September—This is just after kids go back to school and people come back from summer vacations. When people come home and kids go back to school, people start cooking at home a lot

more than in the summertime. This is a great opportunity to offer a first-time-customer promotion.

Other seasonal events can be beneficial to sharpening services that focus in specific areas of the market:

- January and February—slow season for restaurants. It's easier to get a meeting with a restaurant manager when restaurants are slow during this time of the year.
- Summer and fall—great for farmers markets, outdoor public sharpening, community events, and knife/gun shows.
- October and November—big-game hunting season.
- April through October—fishing season.

COLLECT DATA AND REFINE YOUR STRATEGIES

When advertising your sharpening service, it's incredibly important to know which ads and ad platforms worked and which didn't. For this reason, collecting data is crucial. I highly recommend getting set up with Google Analytics. This is a free service that Google provides, and it collects data about the traffic on your website. It's simple to set up. Go to analytics.google.com and register your website. It will provide you with historical information about how many people visited your website, the times and dates they visited your website, and any links they clicked while on your website.

As a business owner, it's a good idea to spend your advertising dollars in the right places. Start by trying out some different strategies you think will work, and then after the ads are done running, refer to your data to see which ads were successful. Invest more into the strategies that were successful, and put less resources into the strategies that were less successful. For instance, if you run a newspaper ad and check in on your analytics data during and after the ad and you don't see a significant spike in web traffic, you can assume that something about your ad didn't work. It could be how it was written, the dates you published it, or simply the fact that people in your area don't read the newspaper. Before you cut out newspaper ads completely, try a couple of different strategies about the information you provide in them and seasonality when you have them published. If you don't see a boost in web traffic after several attempts, then you may consider ditching newspaper ads from your advertising strategy. On the flip side, if you do see a significant boost in web traffic that you can attribute to a specific advertising campaign, put more resources into it and find out how you can make it even better.

If you see traffic increases on your website, but don't do more sales as a result, there may be an issue with your closing strategies on your website. In that scenario it may be good to reevaluate your website's information organization, your pricing, or your overall strategy. When it comes to marketing and advertising, especially when you are first starting out, it's very important to always ask questions and keep refining your strategies until you develop a system that consistently generates sales. Keep good records of your results. Use a simple spreadsheet, and log the results after you run each marketing campaign.

COMPETITION

Many business owners and employees regard their competition as "the enemy." I disagree. I believe competition serves to make business better. Competition inspires creativity and fresh ideas. Though it's important to watch your competitors to see what they are doing, try to keep most of your attention on what you are doing and how you can keep improving your business.

Don't try to poach customers from your competition. If you come across a person who tells you they already use another sharpening service, find out if they are happy with that service. If they are, don't try to persuade the customer to choose you over that service. Everyone has knives. You don't need to aggressively fight to win customers from your competition to create your own success. Your competition has the same right to have a business and to be successful as you do. Your competitors are likely very similar to you. They chose to start a business in this industry to provide a better life for themselves and their families, just the same as you are considering choosing to do.

I once had a customer hire me to sharpen his set of Global knives who had recently had a bad experience with one of my competitors. When I inspected the knives, I found that the edges had been completely dulled. Though they were very dull, the knives were not ruined as the customer thought they could have been. I was familiar with this competitor, and I knew he used a sharpening system that was prone to this type of issue when attempting to sharpen knives made from very hard steel. When knives don't get sharp, some people in the sharpening industry will try to force the knives to become sharp by grinding off a lot of metal from the knife. It was evident to me that this competitor didn't do that. He exercised caution and simply stopped sharpening when the knives didn't get sharp and returned them in a dull condition. I explained this to the customer, taught him a little about the sharpening process and about how the knives became duller, and made sure to note that my competitor could have caused serious damage to the knives but decided to be cautious instead of grinding off more metal. My customer, who was originally furious about the prior sharpening job, was happy I took the time to explain what I thought had happened and grateful the other sharpening service used caution instead of causing irreparable damage to his knives. I sharpened his knives and returned them to him the next day, with incredibly sharp edges. He left me this review:

> *"I thought my beautiful Global knives were ruined by a previous sharpener. I called Kyle and he came out the same day and picked up the knives. The next day he came back, and they were like new! I live thirty minutes from town, and he did not hesitate to make both trips. Highly recommend!! -Todd M*

Don't bad-mouth your competition ever. If a customer has a negative experience with one of your competitors and talks poorly about them, take the high road and try to redirect the conversation. When a customer has a bad experience with one of your competitors, an opportunity is presented because it gives you the chance to earn a new customer and show them how awesome you and your service are. When earning a new customer's business, you can do it without disrespecting your competition. In my opinion, starting off relationships by demonstrating respect and integrity builds a much stronger relationship than showing disrespect toward your competition. Though you should avoid drawing attention to your competition's mistakes, it's important to listen closely to what the customer says about his or her negative experience, so you can learn to not make the same mistakes.

Try to avoid price wars with your competition. If a competitor lowers his or her prices to outbid you, don't lower your prices to outbid them. The race to the bottom ends at zero. If you see a competitor lower his or her prices, I encourage you to reach out to them and ask why. Try to come to an agreement about how much to charge and consider matching your prices together. If you find out they lowered their prices because their business is struggling, consider sharing ideas and try to help each other. The competitor is not the enemy. You could make a friend and learn a lot in the process.

ACTIVELY ENGAGE WITH PEOPLE AND YOUR COMMUNITY

The more actively you get out in your community, meet with and talk to people about your business, and make connections, the more successful your business will become. This is easier said than done. I've found the best way to engage with people and attract positive attention to your business is with generosity and kindness. Go down to your local fire station and tell them you would like to help out by sharpening all the fire fighters' knives. Go to a restaurant and offer to sharpen the knives for free. Promote a free sharpening day and go to a public place and sharpen people's knives free of charge. If you do these types of things just a couple times a year, it will make a world of difference for your business. People will want to give their business to you because people appreciate and want to support businesses who give back to their communities. When you make a great impression on people through generosity, they'll talk about you with their family, friends, and coworkers. Your business will begin to grow very quickly when this happens, and you'll build your business on top of a very strong foundation.

When you set up a sharpener in public, make eye contact with people who walk by your table. Say hello. Talk to them. I have been to so many trade shows and farmers markets and witnessed vendors sitting in their chairs and staring at their phones. It was no surprise that almost nobody approached them or made purchases from them. If you want to do well, try to interact with people—be present. People who engage with their customers make sales. People who stare at their phones don't.

DELIVER AN EXCEPTIONAL CUSTOMER EXPERIENCE

If you want your customers to hire you again and recommend you to their friends, you must deliver an exceptional customer experience. It has been said that in service-type businesses there are three descriptors: good, fast, and cheap—pick two. For example, if a service offers high quality and fast delivery, they won't be cheap. If the service offers high quality and is cheap, they won't be fast. If a service offers fast delivery and is cheap, the quality won't be good. If you can find a way to give high-quality results, fast delivery, and offer your service at a competitive price, you'll stand out from the crowd and people will remember and talk about you.

Word-of-mouth marketing is the strongest form of marketing for small service-type businesses. It should be your top priority to leave a great impression on your customers, so they talk about you. These are the key actions you can take to make sure you are delivering an exceptional customer experience:

- Communicate with your customers promptly. This means checking your email and voicemail regularly and returning emails and calls immediately.
- Be super punctual. Tell your customers when you'll pick up and deliver their knives, and then make sure to be on time. Don't make promises you can't deliver. Make sure you can be where you need to be on time before you make any promises.
- Make your entire ordering process extraordinarily convenient for your customers. This is why I love the pickup and delivery model for sharpening. All customers need to do is make one phone call or place an order on your website, and then you take care of the rest. With this model, the customer doesn't need to pack up their knives and then go out of their way to bring them to you.
- Always make sure knives are incredibly sharp before you deliver them. If a knife gets fairly sharp but isn't as sharp as you know it could be, go back and resharpen it.
- Find little ways to go above and beyond for your customers.

One of my favorite ways to go above and beyond is by repairing minor damage to knives for free. For instance, knives often have a little bit of the tip broken off or minor chips taken out of the blade. You can usually repair these in five minutes or less, and your customers will be super impressed.

To make sure your customers have a way to spread the word about your sharpening service, provide them with multiple business cards when you deliver their knives. I give every one of my customers three business cards so they can keep one and give the other two to friends and neighbors.

If you deliver an excellent customer experience, you'll find that customers tip you. Yes, tipping is customary in the knife-sharpening industry. I find that an average of one in three of my customers leave me a tip, often five dollars or more.

I've been told by many customers that I could charge more for my service. I have chosen not to because I understand the value in the wow factor—an exceptional customer experience that causes a customer to say wow. Increasing my pricing by a dollar per knife would mean an average of five dollars more in my pocket for each customer. By keeping my prices lower and delivering an exceptional experience, I get referrals from many customers, which is worth a lot more to me than the profits from a slight increase in pricing. It's better for my business long term to provide an expedient service with high-quality results at a very reasonable price.

SET A CUSTOMER-ACQUISITION GOAL

You may find it helpful to set a goal for yourself for how many customers you want to acquire within the first three months from your business's launch date, and each month following your launch. The first three months are the most important because it's during this time that your motivation will likely be highest, because you'll be excited about starting your business. That motivation and excitement will translate into energy that you can use to excite others about your business. Lay out a marketing plan to accomplish your goal. Test the waters by trying some of the different marketing strategies discussed in this chapter. When you find strategies that work, devise a plan for how much resources to devote to those strategies to accomplish your goal.

If you succeed in accomplishing your goal, the sense of achievement you'll feel will be all the motivation you need to keep moving the business forward. Be aggressive to accomplish your goal. Be ambitious. Make a promise to yourself that you'll accomplish your goal and do whatever it takes to make sure you don't fall short of it. My sharpening service succeeded because I worked hard to create a buzz around it when I first launched the business. If the business had been slow to get started, knowing myself and what motivates me, it's possible I would have lost motivation to keep the business going.

If you set a goal to acquire forty-five customers in the first three months, all you need to do is find one new customer every other day. That's not difficult to do, considering everyone has knives and is a potential customer. If each of those customers spends an average of twenty-five dollars, you'll have made back a significant portion of the money you spent to get your business started.

CHAPTER 4

ORGANIZATION, STORAGE, AND SAFETY

Very early on in my sharpening service, I made a big mistake because of a lack of organization with knives. I had knives for multiple customers in my possession at a farmers market, and I accidentally mixed up the knives. One knife ended up going to a customer it shouldn't have, and it turned out this knife was worth a few hundred dollars. Because I was at a farmers market, I didn't collect contact information from the other customer who ended up with the knife, so I had no way of tracking him down. This mistake ended up costing me $200, which I had to pay to the customer whose knife I lost. This was a pretty big setback, but through this mistake, I learned a valuable lesson about knife organization and storage and developed a system that would help me to prevent this from happening in the future.

KNIFE ORGANIZATION AND STORAGE

When operating a sharpening service, there are four major organizational and storage mistakes that you could make which could end up costing you a lot of money and seriously damaging your reputation. You need to devise a system to prevent these scenarios from happening.

- Knives get misplaced/lost.
- Knives get mixed up and delivered to the wrong customers.
- Knives get damaged.
- Knives get stolen.

My system for knife storage and organization is simple. I use plastic bins (storage containers) and have strict rules about how I use them. Here are the rules:

- One bin per customer. Never put multiple customers' knives in the same bin.
- Never open more than one bin at a time. When I'm sharpening, I work on one customer's knives at time, and I never open another customer's bin until the first customer's knives are done and placed back in their bin.
- Always put an order form inside the bin with the knives that includes the customer's name, address, and contact information.

As you can see, this is a very simple system, but it works like a charm. I have a total of seven bins. I keep a minimum of three empty bins in my car, so I'm prepared when orders come in during my workday. That way, I don't have to go home to get bins before I start my pickup and delivery route. During the busy season, November and December, I keep all my empty bins in my car. My promise to my customers is to deliver their knives the very next day. If you plan on holding onto knives for longer than one day, you won't cycle bins as quickly as I do, so you'll most likely need more, especially during the busy season.

The bins I use are fourteen inches long, eleven inches wide, three inches deep, and have lids. I do not recommend using bins without lids, especially if your service is pickup/delivery. One of the great things about using bins with lids is it makes traveling with knives safe. The last thing you want to happen is to slam on your brakes and have knives go flying around in your car while you're driving. You can imagine how terrible that could end up being.

Many of my customers already have their knives wrapped in a dish towel, placed in a bag, or placed in a cardboard box when I arrive for the pickup. When the knives are in a bag or a box, I immediately take the knives out of the customer's packaging and place them in my bins. You must stick to a system for the system to be effective. If the knives are neatly bundled in a dish towel, I keep them that way and place the whole bundle in my bin. This will most likely happen to you. Remember: the dish towel is the customer's property, so it must be returned to the customer. There is a benefit to knives being bundled in a dish towel, which is that it makes knives safe from banging into each other while in transit. It also makes the knives safer to handle. For this reason, all my bins have dish towels in them, and I wrap up knives when I receive them. I recommend keeping a large dish towel and a few rubber bands in each one of your bins.

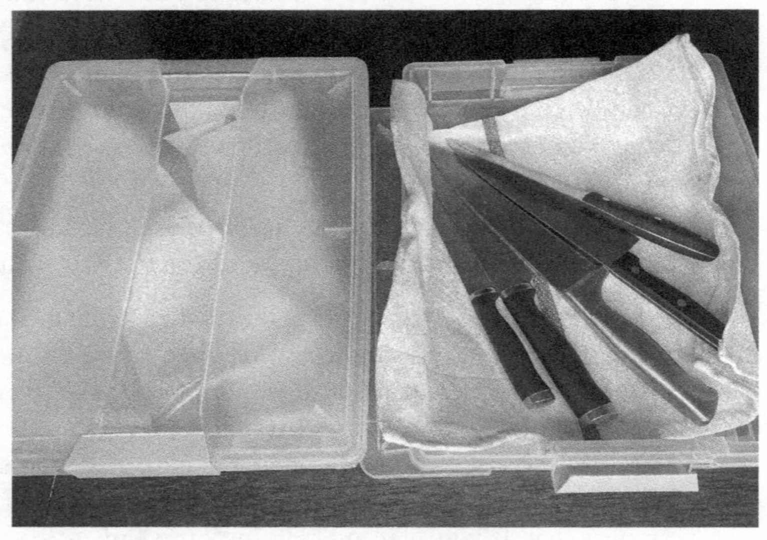

When I open a bin to start sharpening a set of knives, the first thing I do is perform an inspection of all the knives. First, I count the knives to make sure they're all accounted for. I then make a note on the order form about the number of knives that are present. Then I inspect the knives for any damage, and I make notes about what I find. If there's significant preexisting damage to any of the knives, I take a picture of it. Common types of damage include the following:

- broken or damaged handle
- broken blade tip
- bent blade
- chips or dings in the blade's edge
- heavily scratched blade body
- grind marks on the blade body or edge from previous poor sharpening
- presence of rust
- broken or bent pocket clip (pocketknives)
- broken locking mechanism (pocketknives)

Several of these issues can be repaired easily, which will be covered in the second part of this book. You can charge the customer more money to repair knives, but never assume the customer is willing to pay for that. Contact the customer and explain the additional charge before you make repairs and bill for them. If the repair is easy, like a mildly broken or rounded knife tip that takes less than a few minutes to repair, I usually make that repair free of charge to help build a better relationship with my customer.

ORDER FORMS

If you're using an online order form, like a Google Form or one you've built with a different piece of software, you can simply print the completed form and keep it with each of your customer's knives. However, even if you are using an online order form, there may be times when you need to have a blank order form available. For instance, when sharpening at a farmers market or if you take an order over the phone and you're not near a computer, you need to have a form available to take your customer's information. Order forms are an imperative part of staying organized. Here is a sample of a simple order form. You're welcome to use it.

<table>
<tr><th colspan="3">KNIFE-SHARPENING ORDER FORM</th></tr>
<tr><td colspan="3">CUSTOMER INFORMATION</td></tr>
<tr><td colspan="2">Customer Name:</td><td>Phone Number:</td></tr>
<tr><td colspan="3">Street Address:</td></tr>
<tr><td colspan="2">City</td><td>State: / Zip:</td></tr>
<tr><td colspan="3">Email Address:</td></tr>
<tr><td colspan="2">Pickup Date/Time:</td><td>Delivery Date/Time:</td></tr>
<tr><td colspan="3">KNIFE INFORMATION</td></tr>
<tr><td colspan="3">Total Knives:</td></tr>
<tr><td>Knife Type</td><td>Length</td><td>Notes</td></tr>
<tr><td></td><td></td><td></td></tr>
<tr><td></td><td></td><td></td></tr>
<tr><td></td><td></td><td></td></tr>
<tr><td></td><td></td><td></td></tr>
<tr><td></td><td></td><td></td></tr>
</table>

SAFETY WHEN EXCHANGING KNIVES

Sharp knives are inherently dangerous if not handled correctly, especially to those who are not used to handling very sharp knives. You will find that many of your customers' knives have not been sharpened in years, and the edges of their knives are quite dull. People get used to not being cautious around their knives because they are not afraid of them, so it's very important that you teach your customers to handle their knives with care. Make a point to tell your customers how sharp their knives are and tell them to use caution.

When you deliver knives to your customers, try to avoid handing the knives directly to your customers with the edges exposed. It's better if the knives are in knife sleeves or edge protectors, or wrapped in a dish towel, paper towels, or durable bags. Try to avoid placing knives directly in your customers' hands. It's best if you place them all on a table or counter for your customer and let them pick the knives up themselves. If you must hand a knife directly to a customer, hand the knife to them so they can grab the knife's handle. Hold the blade with the back side of the knife (the spine of the knife) facing inward toward your palm, and the edge facing away from your hand. Never hand more than one knife at a time to a customer unless the knives are very securely bundled together. Make sure the customer has a firm grip before you let go.

CHAPTER 5

TAXES, ACCOUNTING, AND FINANCING

BENJAMIN FRANKLIN SAID, "IN THIS world nothing is certain but death and taxes." Unfortunately, as a small-business owner, you'll need to do some light accounting work, and you'll have to pay taxes. Fortunately, thanks to services like TurboTax and QuickBooks, doing your taxes has never been easier. This chapter is written for first-time business owners. If you already have experience with taxes, accounting, and financing, feel free to skip ahead to the next chapter.

Tax laws vary from state to state, and they also change fairly frequently. I'm not a tax professional. The information in this chapter is meant to provide you with an illustration of examples but should not be used in preparation of any tax filings or take the place of advice from actual tax professionals. Consult with a tax professional or certified public accountant when filing your taxes.

TAX FILING STATUS

You are required by law to report any income if your annual income for your business exceeds $400. When you start your business and register it with the IRS, you'll need to choose a tax filing status. There are several to choose from:

- Sole proprietorship—This business structure is the simplest and most common tax filing status for small businesses. Taxes are passed through the business and onto the owner. The owner assumes all liabilities for the business.
- Partnership—This structure functions similarly to a sole propri-

etorship, but the business's profits and tax liabilities are shared by two or more owners.

- Limited liability company (LLC)—This structure combines pass-through taxation with the limited liability of a corporation.
- Corporation—A corporation is an organization that operates as its own entity, separate from any owners.

If you don't have a partner and you plan on using your sharpening service as a side business, I recommend filing as a sole proprietorship. It will make filing taxes at the end of the year a lot easier for you. If you aren't intimately familiar with tax filing statuses, you should consult with a certified public accountant before making your decision.

Once you've chosen your tax filing status, you'll need to register your business with the state you live in. Business registration is done by your state's office of the Secretary of State. You can usually register your business online on the Secretary of State's website. The filing fees vary from state to state.

After you have registered your business with your state, obtain an employer identification number (EIN), also called a federal tax ID number, from the IRS. You can do this online. If filing as a sole proprietor, all you'll need is the official name of your business and your social security number. Here is where you can apply:

https://www.irs.gov/businesses/small-businesses-self-employed/apply-for-an-employer-identification-number-ein-online

After you register your business with the federal IRS, you also need to obtain a state tax ID number so you can pay local taxes. The process for how to do this varies from state to state. Search in Google for how to obtain a tax ID number in your state.

As a sole proprietor, there are three different types of taxes you'll need to pay:

- Income tax—the profit your business makes (income minus expenses) is taxable just like income from a job. This is payable once annually.
- Self-employment tax—This is an additional tax that you must pay as the owner of a sole proprietorship. It does not include income tax. This is strictly to withhold Social Security and Medicare taxes,

just like the withholdings on a paycheck from an employer. This is payable to the IRS quarterly.

- Gross receipts tax, aka sales tax—When you collect sales tax from your customers, you must give those taxes to your state. This is payable to your state on a monthly basis, if you live in a state that collects sales tax.

Taxes are no doubt confusing, especially if this is your first time owning a business. Again, you'll find it helpful to consult with a certified public accountant so you can get a better understanding of how taxes work, specifically in your state. It may also be worth hiring a freelance bookkeeper to keep your books and file taxes for you once a month.

KEEP GREAT RECORDS

You'll need to keep a record of every sales transaction. You can do this in a spreadsheet, or you can use QuickBooks Online. QuickBooks will cost you approximately thirty dollars per month, and I highly recommend it. It's easy to use and makes filing taxes at the end of the year a lot easier.

I recommend using Square Point of Sale as a cash register. Every time you sharpen knives and deliver them to a customer, write up the sale in Square and select which type of payment the customer used within the Square app. If you do this, there will be an electronic record of your transactions, and you won't have to go back and manually enter your sales into QuickBooks later. Square Point of Sale integrates directly with QuickBooks, making record keeping extraordinarily easy. Make sure to integrate Square Point of Sale with QuickBooks as soon as you set up your accounts.

In addition to keeping records of your sales and income, you should keep excellent records of your expenses. At the end of the year, you'll owe taxes on your business's profits, which is income minus expenses. If you haven't recorded all your expenses, you'll owe a lot more in taxes. Tax deductible expenses include, but are not limited to, the following:

- Mileage expense on your vehicle. Download the QuickBooks Self Employed app for your phone so you can easily track your mileage when you drive. The miles you put on your vehicle for any business-related trip are tax deductible. You can write off 57.5 cents (2020 federal rate) from your taxes for every mile that you drive for your business. For example, when you drive a ten-mile pickup/delivery route, $5.75 will be tax deductible at the end of the year. Over the course of a year, this turns into a big number.

- Gas—at the end of the year, you'll be able to expense either your mileage or the amount you paid for gas. If you plug both numbers into TurboTax, it will tell you if you'll benefit more to deduct your gas expense or your mileage expense.
- Office supplies—paper, pens, ink, a new computer, a new phone for your business, and so on are all tax deductible.
- Marketing expenses—every dollar you spend on marketing, whether it's for your logo, your website, social media ads or newspaper ads, is tax deductible.
- Equipment—all your sharpening equipment, including your initial expenses and your costs to replace any items that year, can be deducted from your taxes.
- Work-related educational expenses—if you pay for any education to help you grow your knowledge and build your business, you'll most likely be able to deduct those expenses from your taxes. For instance, you can deduct what you paid for this book.
- Home office space—if you set up an area of your house to use for sharpening and as an office for your business, you can deduct a percentage of your rent or mortgage as a business expense. For instance, if your home office accounts for 10 percent of the square footage of your house, and you pay $1,500 per month in rent ($18,000 annually), you can deduct $1,800 from your taxes.
- Incidental expenses—if you damage a customer's knife and need to replace or pay the customer for it, the amount you pay is tax deductible.

Keeping track of all your expenses isn't always easy, especially when some of those expenses are monthly subscriptions that are automatically charged to your credit card or checking account. To make keeping track of expenses easier, I recommend setting up a checking account for your business that's separate from your personal checking account and setting up a business credit card.

GET A CREDIT CARD FOR YOUR BUSINESS

Opening a credit card account specifically for your business has some great benefits. If you use your credit card to make all the purchases for your business each month, you can simply look at your account statement to find all your expenses for your business. The benefit of using a credit card to do this versus using a debit card is that you get to take advantage of the rewards that credit card companies offer. For instance, depending on the credit card you decided to go with, you can collect travel miles for each of your purchases, or you can collect cash back.

When shopping for a credit card, you may consider choosing a card that offers 0 percent APR for the first twelve or more months. You can then use that card to finance a lot of your start-up costs instead of using cash from your savings, and you won't pay anything in interest for the first year.

If you decide to finance your start-up costs with a credit card, make sure to pay off the card before the 0 percent APR introductory period expires. You don't want to get caught paying interest. If you use your credit card for your expenses every month, pay off the card every month so you don't pay interest on money borrowed.

FINANCIAL DISCIPLINE

When you deliver knives and the customer hands you a twenty-dollar bill, it can be very tempting to put it in your wallet with the rest of your cash to be spent on personal expenses like groceries. When you do this, accounting for your business's revenue and cash balance becomes very difficult. I recommend keeping your business's cash, and any other forms of payment, separate from your personal money. When you make deliveries, sharpen at farmers markets, or however you decide to conduct your business, keep a cash bag with you and put all the payments you receive into it. Once or twice a week, go to your bank and deposit all your business's earnings into your business's checking account. If you would like to withdraw money from your business to use for personal expenses, make the withdrawal a separate transaction so it shows up with the full amount you withdrew in your bank account summary. You'll need to log the withdrawal in your accounting software, and it's easier to do this if you can simply see the total amount of the withdrawal in your transaction history.

Set up all your payment methods so they're linked with your business's checking account. If you accept payments from your customers via

Square, PayPal, or Venmo, make sure they are all linked to your business's checking account. Every month pay your business's credit card bill with your business's checking account. If you do it this way, you'll have a lot better visibility into the finances of your business, and accounting will be much easier.

KEEP A CASH RESERVE

At the end of the year, you'll owe income taxes on your profits. If you withdraw all of your business's revenue and don't have enough left over at the end of the year to pay taxes, you'll regret it. I always recommend keeping 20 percent of your business's revenue in your bank account. I also recommend keeping three times your monthly expenses in your bank account, plus a buffer for miscellaneous expenses on hand. If your business has some slow months, you'll still have expenses that will need to be paid each month, and you'll want cash on hand to pay those expenses. This is an example of how the math works:

> January income: $1,200. Reserve 20 percent for taxes = $240.
>
> February income: $1,400. Reserve 20 percent for taxes = $280.
>
> After these two months, you should have $520 in your bank account reserved for taxes.
>
> Monthly expenses: $50 per month in automatic payments for your website, QuickBooks, and so on, $100 monthly marketing and advertising expense. Total = $150 per month.
>
> Total to keep on hand in case business slows down: Three times monthly expenses = $450.
>
> I like to keep $500 on hand for miscellaneous expenses.

If you add these three factors up, the total cash reserve in your bank account after January and February should be $1,470. You would then keep adding 20 percent of your revenue to your cash reserve at the end of each month.

THIS IS WHAT IT WOULD LOOK LIKE FOR THE ENTIRE YEAR:

	Revenue	**20% Reserve**	**Total Reserved in Bank Account**
Total Reserve for Monthly and Misc. Expenses			$950
January	$1,200	$240	$1,190
February	$1,400	$280	$1,470
March	$900	$180	$1,650
April	$1,100	$220	$1,870
May	$700	$140	$2,010
June	$800	$160	$2,170
July	$1,200	$240	$2,410
August	$600	$120	$2,530
September	$900	$180	$2,710
October	$1,400	$280	$2,990
November	$2,100	$420	$3,410
December	$1,200	$240	$3,650

PART 2
KNIFE SHARPENING

CHAPTER 6

BASIC SHARPENING PRINCIPLES

To learn how to sharpen knives, you must first learn the vocabulary and jargon used in the knife world. Begin by familiarizing yourself with the anatomy of a knife and the unique word used to describe each individual part of a knife.

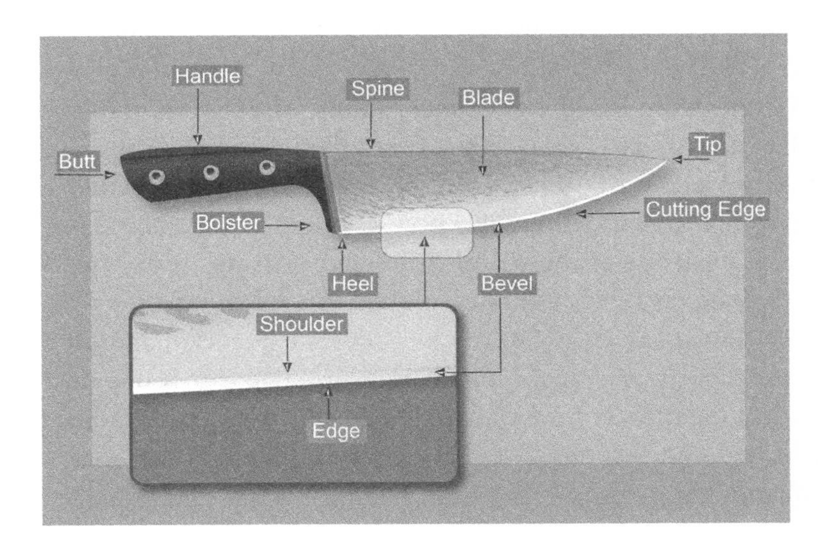

KNIFE SHARPENING GLOSSARY OF TERMS

Abrasive—Abrasives are what we use to remove material from a knife to reshape and refine the edge until it is sharp. There are many abrasive mediums, like sandpaper and diamond sharpening stones, and there are usually many levels of sizes within each abrasive medium.

- **Coarse** (abrasive)—Describes an abrasive made of large particles that remove material quickly.
- **Fine** (abrasive)—Describes an abrasive made of small particles that do not remove material as quickly as a coarse abrasive, but create a more refined edge finish.

Edge Finish—Describes the intentional final result of the edge after sharpening and level of refinement that has been achieved. For example, a "toothy" edge versus a "polished" edge.

- **Toothy** (edge)—An edge that has been finished by coarser abrasives. An edge that has a toothy finish will have microscopic teeth at the edge's apex.
- **Polished** (edge)—An edge that has been well refined and has a crisp surface, without teeth, at the edge's apex.

Grit—Indicates the grade of fineness of an abrasive. When comparing grit sizes, the larger number is indicative of a finer abrasive—200 grit is finer than 100 grit.

Micron—Also called a micrometer, a micron is a unit of measure. One micron equals 1/1,000 of a millimeter. Like a grit scale, microns are used to indicate the fineness of an abrasive. This measurement for defining fineness examines the overall size of an abrasive particle or the size of the scratch a single abrasive particle will create on a surface. For example, a one-micron diamond stone includes thousands of one-micron diamond particles, and each of those particles will create a scratch in the edge that is one-micron wide. Opposite of the grit scale, when comparing micron sizes, the smaller number is the finer abrasive—one micron is finer than two microns.

Edge—The part of the knife on which abrasives have removed material, so a fine point has been formed.

- **Apex** (of an edge)—This is the part of the edge that pierces into the object being cut—the tippy-top of the edge.
- **Shoulder** (of an edge)—This is the part of the edge where the body of the blade meets the edge. The edge is cut into the blade at

a different angle than the angle of the body of the blade, and the shoulder of the edge is where that change in angle occurs.

Edge Grind—Describes the intentional shape of the edge. There are three common edge grinds, which will be discussed later.

Edge Durability—Describes the longevity of the lifespan of an edge. For example, an edge that is not durable will become dull more quickly.

Knife sharpening is all about geometry. To simplify the geometrical concepts and make them easier to understand, it's helpful to visualize an edge in two dimensions instead of three. Many of the graphics in this book are two-dimensional. They represent an upward-facing edge from the perspective of viewing the cross section of a knife.

Sharpening knives is not complicated once you understand the basic principles of how an edge is built and the possible structures of an edge that make it either sharp or dull. A sharp edge is most often shaped like a triangle. A dull edge can look like either a triangle with a blunt top, a rounded top, or a bent top.

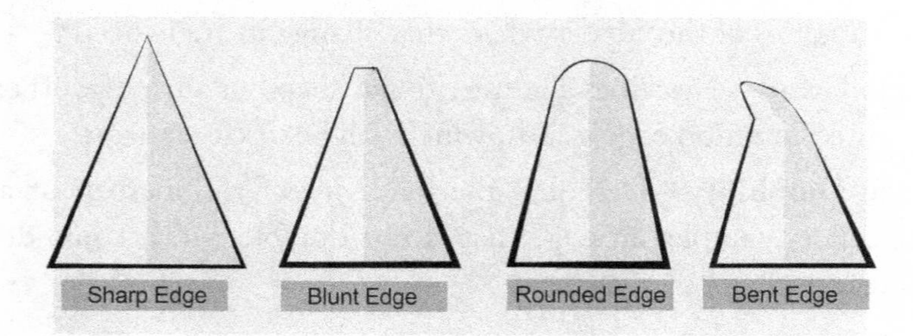

A knife sharpener's job is to cut away the excess material from an edge until a pointed top is formed. To do this, you must use abrasives to remove material from the blade.

To create a perfectly shaped edge, you must make many passes with the abrasive against the knife's edge to remove material, and each pass with the abrasive should make contact with the edge at the same angle as the previous pass. To accomplish this, it's helpful to use a sharpening system that helps you control the sharpening angle. Without a guide for the abrasives, the person doing the sharpening must hold the knife or abrasive perfectly, so the abrasive and the knife contact each other at the exact same angle with each stroke, which is incredibly difficult. Without accomplishing the same angle with each stroke, it's likely the edge will not become sharp and the edge's structure will not be sound, causing the knife to become duller more quickly.

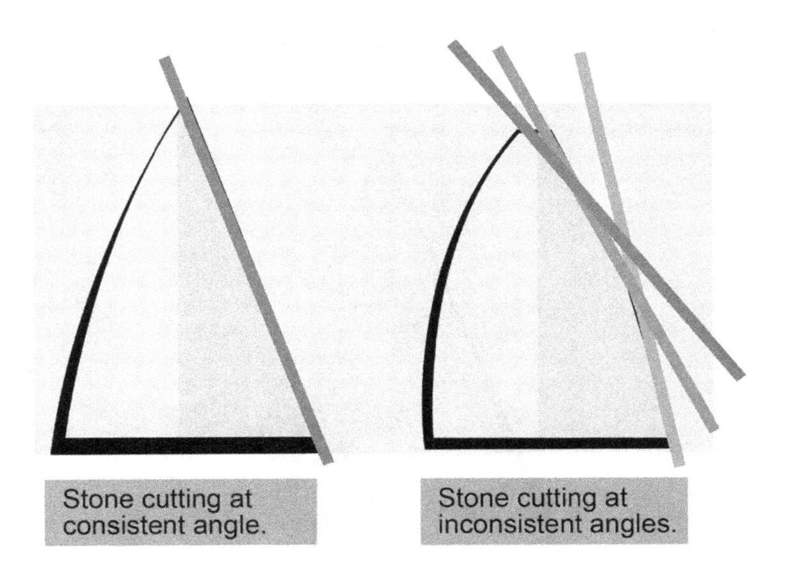

Knives require a wide range of sharpening angles from one knife to the next, depending on how the knife was built or how it was previously sharpened. For instance, Japanese-style knives usually require a more acute sharpening angle than German-style knives.

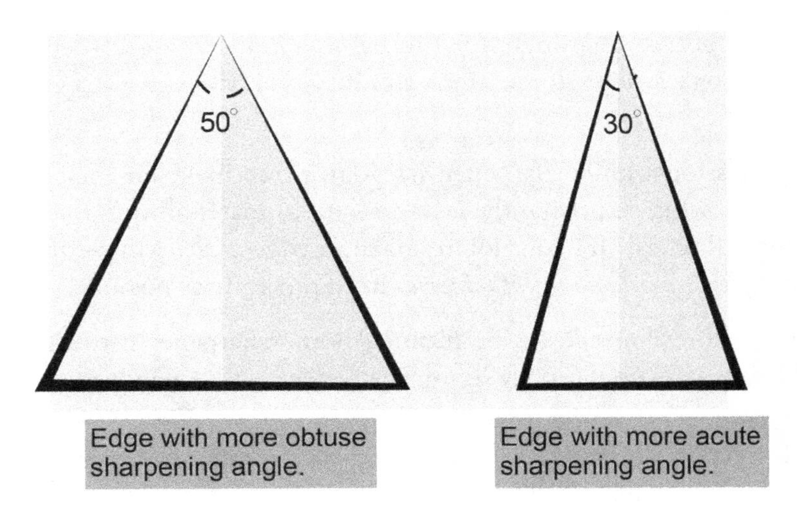

In the knife world, there are two methods for discussing sharpening angles: individual side angle, and inclusive angle. The inclusive angle is always the sum of the two individual sides. For instance, if the individual angle on each side of the edge is 20 degrees, the inclusive angle will be 40 degrees.

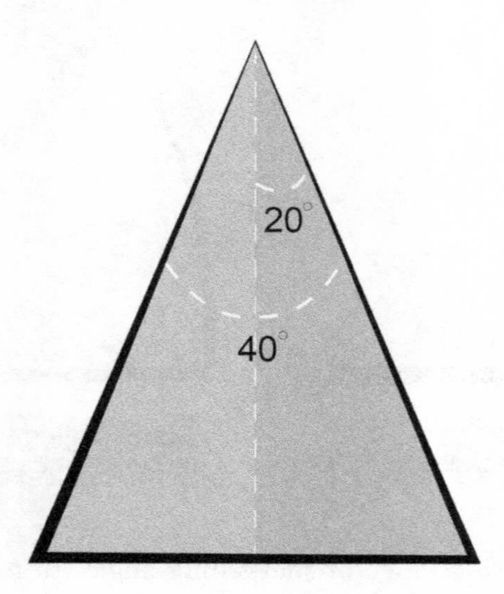

The lowest sharpening angle I have ever seen on a knife is 8 degrees per side. The widest angle I have ever seen is 38 degrees per side. Most knives require sharpening angles within the range of 15 to 30 degrees per side. As a rule, knives with more acute edge angles will be sharper than knives with more obtuse edge angles. For instance, a knife with a 15-degree-per-side edge angle will be sharper than a knife with a 30-degree-per-side edge angle.

As a professional knife sharpener, it's your job to make an edge as sharp as possible, while removing the least amount of material from the knife as possible. I'll repeat. It's your job to make an edge *as sharp as possible* while removing the *least amount of material* from the knife as possible.

There are three mistakes a professional knife sharpener can make that would cause an unnecessary amount of metal to be removed from the edge.

1. They could use too narrow of a sharpening angle, removing too much material from the shoulder of the edge.
2. They could use too wide of a sharpening angle, removing too much material from the apex of the edge.

3. They could remove too much material from the entire edge, even if sharpening at the correct angle, by spending too much time grinding at the edge.

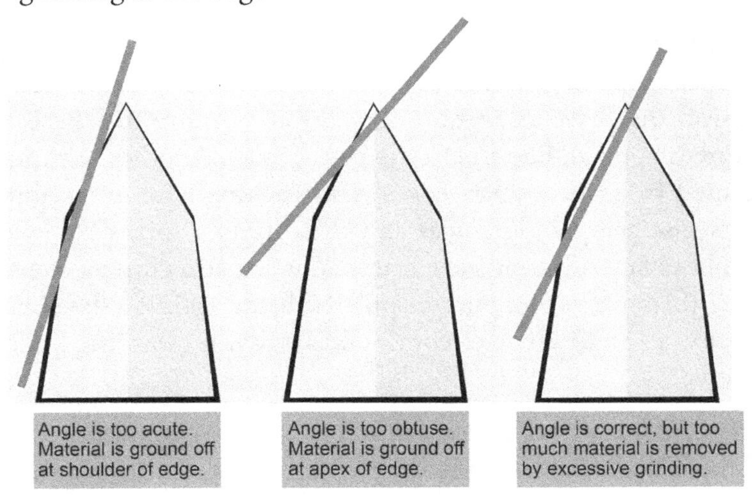

To achieve the best results in the shortest amount of time spent sharpening, in which the knife becomes incredibly sharp and a minimal amount of material is removed, you need to match the preexisting edge angle as best you can. The right equipment and technique to accomplish this will be covered in detail later in this chapter and the next chapter.

EDGE GRINDS

An edge grind describes the overall shape of an edge. There are three types of edge grinds that you should be aware of: V grinds, convex grinds, and chisel grinds.

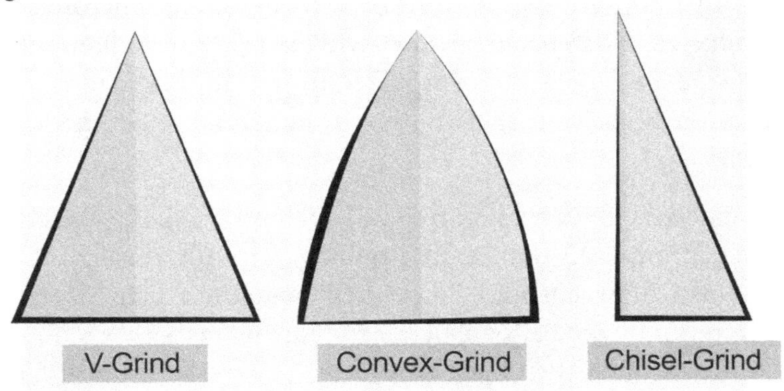

A V grind is shaped exactly as it sounds. Flat surfaces on each side of the knife meet to form the shape of a V. V grinds are usually created by flat abrasives.

A convex grind is an edge that has outward curves on each side of the knife, which eventually meet and form a point. Convex grinds are created by abrasives that have an inward curve or an abrasive that flexes inward as pressure is applied, like an electric belt grinder. Another technique that can be used to create convex edges is sharpening with a flat abrasive at several precise sharpening angles and then using a soft, flexible abrasive like leather to smooth over the corners. You can also create a convex edge by rolling the knife as you push or pull the blade against a flat abrasive, so the sharpening angle changes continuously as you move the knife across the abrasive.

A chisel grind describes an edge that has a bevel on one side, and the other side of the blade is flat. Because the flat side has a zero-degree sharpening angle, the inclusive edge angle will be the same as the angle of the beveled side of the knife. This means these types of edges can be incredibly sharp due to the extremely low inclusive edge angle. Chisel grind edges are found on some pocketknives, and are common among high-end Japanese kitchen cutlery, like sushi knives.

EDGE FINISHES

The coarseness of the abrasive you use to finish a knife will determine the final cutting ability and performance of the knife. Different edge finishes are better for different cutting tasks. For instance, an edge that has been finished with a 600-grit diamond stone will have larger microscopic teeth than an edge that has been finished with a 1,500-grit diamond stone. When an edge has larger microscopic teeth, we call this a "toothy" finish. The coarser the abrasive is that you use to finish the knife, the bigger the teeth will be.

A toothy edge acts like a miniature saw, which is beneficial when the knife is used for cutting tasks that require pulling the knife through the object being cut (aka draw cutting), like when opening a box. More refined edges with fewer or no teeth are better for cutting tasks that require pushing the knife through the object being cut (aka push cutting), like when chopping vegetables.

It's hard to know exactly what customers will use their knives for, or how they will use them, so I believe it's best to finish the majority of knives with an edge that is well refined, but also has small micro teeth. This balance is accomplished by finishing most knives with an abrasive within a range of 1,000 to 2,000 grit.

If you provide sharpening services to customers with high-end collectible knives, your customers may ask you to create a "mirror edge." This edge finish is exactly what it sounds like–it's shiny and reflective like a mirror. This type of edge isn't very effective for many cutting tasks, but it looks super cool. Tasks a highly polished edge are effective for include shaving, whittling, and any other task that involves push-cutting where the edge is pushing straight into the object being cut, without a drawing motion. If you would like to offer these types of edges to your customers, be prepared to use many more abrasives and spend thirty-plus minutes sharpening each knife.

WHY KNIVES BECOME DULL

Knives become dull for two reasons: pressure and friction. When used, pressure is applied by the knife user to force the knife through the object being cut. The more pressure is applied, the more force pushes against the knife's edge, which causes it to become misshapen. As the knife cuts through the object, friction is created and allows metal particles to be pulled away from the edge's apex, causing dullness. When a knife is duller, more pressure is required to force the knife through the object, which further dulls the edge. Pressure can have two effects on an edge. It can smoosh the edge, causing the apex of the edge to become blunt or rounded, or it can cause the edge to bend over to one side. The latter is more common with softer steels.

There are several main mistakes knife owners make that will expedite the dulling process: not using a cutting board, storing knives loosely in a drawer where they can bang into each other and other objects, using an unnecessary amount of pressure when using the knife, or putting knives in a dishwasher.

The prior sharpening job and the structure of the edge also play a big part in how quickly a knife will become dull. A perfect triangular structure is very strong, and a wavy structure is not. A wavy edge is created by sharpening the knife at inconsistent sharpening angles and inconsistent pressure at different areas of the edge. When an edge is wavy, the apex is prone to being pushed over when the knife is used, which causes it to become dull.

The hardness of the steel the knife is made from also plays a large role in how long the knife will stay sharp. Harder, higher-quality steel will hold an edge longer than softer, lower quality steels.

SHARPENING PRODUCTS

I have seen $200-plus sharpening systems sitting on the counters at my customer's houses, and they were still paying me to sharpen their knives. Why? Sharpening systems designed for convenience and speed hardly ever produce great results. The sharpening systems that produce better results are often priced higher and require learning a new skill. The combination of those two factors make those better sharpening systems undesirable for many people. However, a lot of people appreciate incredibly sharp knives and want to keep their knives in great condition for a long time, which is why there is a market for skilled sharpening services.

I encourage you to check out as many knife-sharpening products as you can so you can develop firsthand knowledge of them. People will ask you about these products, and the more knowledgeable you are, the more your clients will trust you, which will help you to build lasting relationships with them. Knife-sharpening products are sold in many places. Knife stores, kitchen stores, hardware stores, Williams-Sonoma, Bass Pro Shops, or any other kitchen supply or outdoor supply store carries a selection of them. Go talk to a salesperson and ask them to show you different models of knife sharpeners.

Many companies have realized how big the market potential for sharpening is, which is why so many sharpening products exist. There are hundreds of options for sharpening products, ranging from $2 carbide pull-through sharpeners to $2,000-plus sharpening machines. As a sharpening service owner, or any business owner, it's important for you to know what you're up against so you can explain to your customers why the solution you offer is superior. We can break most sharpening products down into the five categories described below.

PULL-THROUGH SHARPENERS

These sharpeners utilize a cross section of an abrasive that forms a V shape. You simply pull the knife through the V and the abrasive carves away the excess metal on the edge of the knife. These sharpeners are inexpensive to produce so they can be made available to consumers at a low price. They work best when you need to put a functional edge on a very dull blade. The problem with these sharpeners is they usually remove too much metal from the knife by sharpening at an angle that's different than the knife's edge angle, and they produce a result that looks like ripped metal when you examine the edge under magnification. Knives sharpened by these sharpening systems become dull very quickly, so you end up sharpening and removing more material from the knife more frequently.

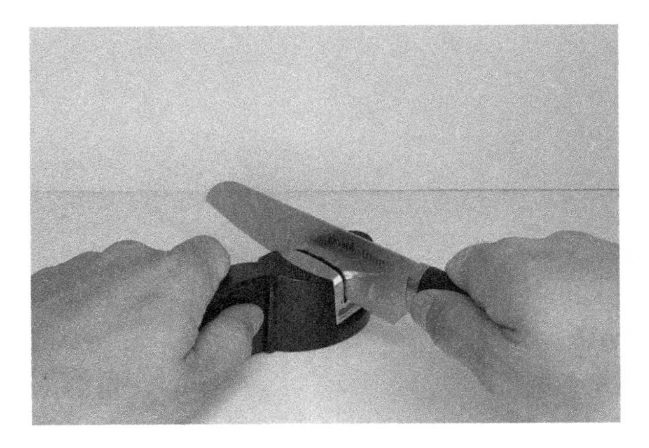

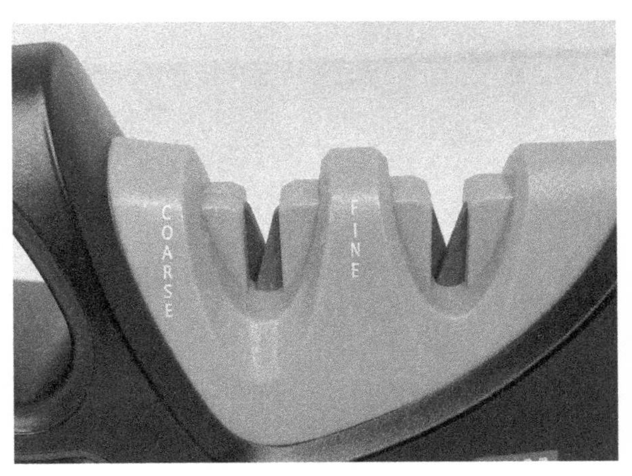

ELECTRIC PULL-THROUGH SHARPENERS

These sharpening machines work similarly to the nonmechanical pull-through sharpeners described above and produce similar results. Instead of a stationary V-shaped abrasive cross section, they utilize small abrasive disks or belts that remove metal from the knife as you pull the knife through the sharpener. Some have just one abrasive, and some have a progression of abrasives side by side. To use these sharpeners, simply pull the knife through the coarsest abrasive first and finish on the finest abrasive. The benefit of these sharpeners is they're very convenient to use. However, the results they produce aren't great, and you end up using them a lot more than desirable, which takes off too much metal and can ruin knives in a short time. They too can have significant issues with sharpening geometry.

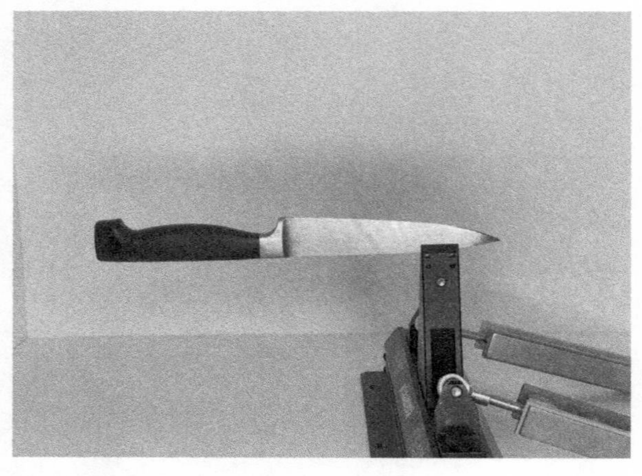

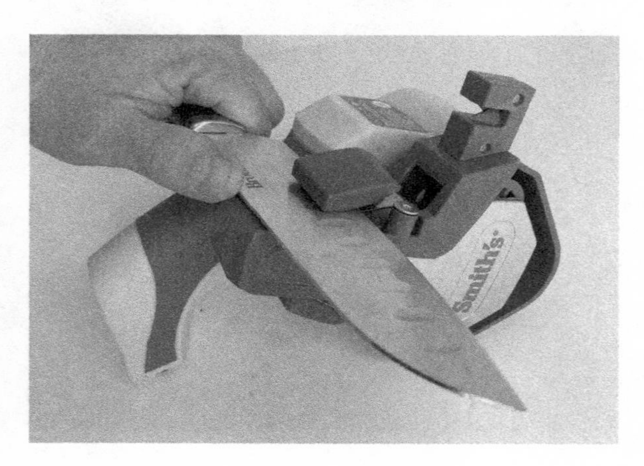

FREEHAND SHARPENING STONES

These are common sharpening stones with no mechanical parts or angle guides. Simply push your knife against the stone or vice-versa. Freehand sharpening stones can be made from many abrasive types, including natural stones, diamond stones, whetstones, silicon carbide stones, aluminum oxide stones, and more. I have seen people produce incredible results sharpening freehand, but it can take years of practice, and it usually requires a lot of time and patience on each knife to produce great results.

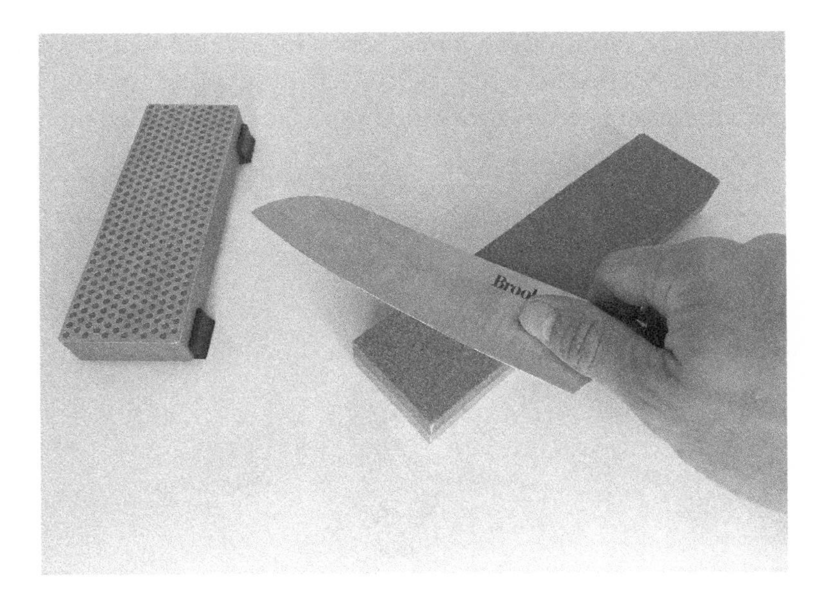

ELECTRIC BELT AND WHEEL SHARPENERS

These are the choice of many conventional sharpening services and knife manufacturers, but I do not recommend them unless you are very well practiced. There are many different styles to these sharpeners. To use them, hold the edge of the knife against the abrasive belt or spinning abrasive wheel and move the knife across the abrasive so it contacts the entire edge of the knife. Using these sharpeners is risky because you can remove a lot of material from the blade very quickly and do irreparable damage to a blade in an instant. The advantage of these sharpening systems is they are fast. If you would like to start a sharpening service that focuses on high volume at low prices, I would choose an electric system and spend a lot of time learning how to use it well.

ANGLE-GUIDED PRECISION SHARPENING SYSTEMS

Precision sharpening systems consist of a main sharpener body that holds the knife, and guided abrasives that sharpen the knife at a user-chosen angle setting. You can decide which angle to use for the knife, set the angle on the sharpener, and let the sharpener guide the abrasive as you push the abrasive against the edge of the knife. These systems can be highly effective at creating excellent results while removing a minimal amount of material from the blade. However, there are many to choose from and you get what you pay for. Though they're not as fast as electric sharpening systems, they can produce much better results and you can achieve excellent results with a lot less practice. This type of sharpening system is my preference and recommendation, especially for smaller sharpening services.

THE RIGHT EQUIPMENT FOR A SMALL SHARPENING SERVICE

Knife sharpening is all about geometry. To achieve the sharpest results while removing the least amount of material from an edge, you need to use a sharpening system that offers great adjustability to the sharpening angle. If you can't adjust a sharpening angle, you'll undoubtedly sharpen knives at angles that don't match the knives, which will remove too much material and produce less-than-optimal results.

If you're someone who's just getting into sharpening, I recommend choosing a sharpening system that produces incredible results by delivering precise angle control, doesn't remove too much material from knives, and is easy to learn how to use.

It's for these reasons that I highly recommend precision, manual knife-sharpening equipment. Electric sharpening systems run the risk of damaging knives by removing too much material, and they don't offer great angle control. Other types of manual sharpening systems, like pull-through sharpeners, don't offer enough angle control to effectively match the sharpening geometry of each unique knife.

There are many companies that produce precision sharpening equipment. Edge Pro, TSPROF, and KME are companies that all make good sharpening systems. However, in my opinion they all have one major design issue that makes them an inferior choice for a sharpening service: only one side of the knife can be sharpened at a time. To use them, you have to sharpen one side of the knife with your coarse abrasive, then flip the knife over and sharpen the other side, then switch to your next finest abrasive, flip the knife over again, and continue like this until you reach the final abrasive. Though each of these sharpeners can produce excellent results, I believe the sharpening process simply takes too long, especially for a sharpening service.

Wicked Edge sharpeners are the only sharpening systems in existence that allow for high-precision sharpening and sharpen both sides of the knife, without having to flip the knife. In short, it takes about half the time to sharpen a knife compared to other precision sharpening systems.

Aside from not requiring a power source, which is very beneficial to mobile sharpening businesses—and better for global warming—there are three main advantages to choosing a precision manual sharpening system versus an electric system: they offer more precision and are more easily controlled, they are easier to learn how to use, and there's a significantly lower chance of removing too much material and damaging blades. Many knife-sharpening services prefer to use electric sharpening systems because of the time reduction to sharpen each knife. I disagree with that approach, especially for a part-time sharpening service. Once you're proficient with a Wicked Edge sharpener, which only takes practicing on about twenty knives to learn well, you'll be able to sharpen a knife in about five minutes.

You'll likely produce much better results with a Wicked Edge sharpening system than you could with an electric sharpening system, and you'll achieve excellent results without removing an unacceptable amount of material from the knife.

Before making the commitment to choose Wicked Edge for your sharpening equipment, I encourage you to check out all the other options. As a business owner, you should do your due diligence before you make a purchase. Do your research, watch videos, read reviews, and compare options. If you decide to choose Wicked Edge, read on. The remainder of the book is about which specific model to choose, how it works, and how to learn how to use it.

CHAPTER 7

YOUR SHARPENING EQUIPMENT

I'm a big believer in the phrase "fail fast, fail cheap." What this means is that you should never heavily invest time or money into a concept until the concept has been proven. That way, you can easily recover losses if the concept fails, and you won't invest time in a failing strategy when your time could be better spent focusing on a strategy that works. For this reason, I strongly believe in limiting your financial exposure when you're first getting started. Start with the basic equipment that you'll need to start making money. Once you've proved that you can be successful, look for ways you can expand your success by adding capabilities to your sharpening service or finding ways to reduce your costs.

CHOOSING A WICKED EDGE SHARPENING SYSTEM

Wicked Edge offers several sharpener models. All of them, regardless of their price points, can produce the exact same results, provided the same abrasives are used with each one. The difference between them has to do mainly with their ease of use and versatility. For instance, the higher-end models have a knife-clamping mechanism that's operated with a lever, whereas the lower-end systems' clamps are operated with an Allen key or Allen wrench. Some of the sharpener models have wider angle ranges, like 13 to 35 degrees per side, compared to other models that have a more limited range of 15 to 30 degrees per side.

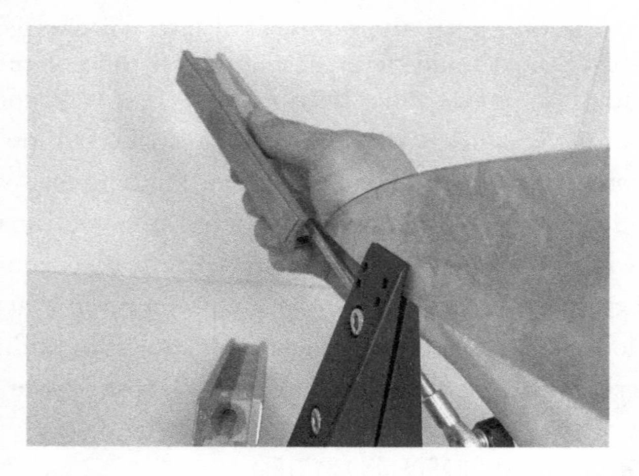

With “fail fast, fail cheap” in mind, I believe the low-end, portable-sharpener option that Wicked Edge offers is the best sharpener to get started with if you are starting a sharpening service as a side job. As previously stated, you’ll achieve the same results with the most affordable Wicked Edge sharpener as you’ll with the most expensive Wicked Edge sharpener, provided that you use the same abrasives to sharpen the knife. All Wicked Edge sharpener models are very well made from aluminum and stainless-steel parts, so even the most affordable sharpener will hold up under very heavy use.

The primary reason I believe the lower-end Wicked Edge knife sharpener is the right sharpener to start a small sharpening service is its price point and the value you get at that price. You can start your sharpening service for a much lower investment than if you choose a higher-end Wicked Edge model. The second reason I recommend starting with the low-end sharpener is the portability it offers that is unmatched by any other Wicked Edge sharpener model. If you do decide that you want a high-end Wicked Edge model after you prove your business can be successful, you can purchase it knowing that the portable sharpener will still have a purpose in your business. A higher-end Wicked Edge model, like the Generation 3 Pro Sharpener, which is designed for faster knife clamping and rapid angle adjustment, will save you time in sharpening. If you purchase it later on, you'll have one sharpener that stays at home or your place of business, which would be your primary sharpener, and another that you can keep in your vehicle or bring with you to give sharpening demonstrations or sharpen customers' knives wherever you are.

This is what I do for my sharpening service. I have a high-end Wicked Edge sharpener that stays on my sharpening desk at home, and a portable Wicked Edge sharpener that travels with me in my vehicle. The strategy is simple—start your business for a lower initial out-of-pocket investment, and then if you want to cut your sharpening time down, upgrade to a

Wicked Edge model that will save you time with the money you make from the first sharpener. You won't take a loss on the original sharpener you purchased, because it will still be valuable to your business. I believe the low-end, portable Wicked Edge sharpener is the only Wicked Edge sharpener model that holds its value as well when you introduce another Wicked Edge sharpener model into your business because of its portability and the versatility to your sharpening service that portability provides. If you have two stationary Wicked Edge models, one will collect dust and not be of much value to you.

The above recommendation and strategy about which sharpener model to choose is designed for people starting sharpening services as a side business. However, if you're someone who likes to swing for the fence on the first pitch, and you've done your market research ahead of time, like you should, and you have a good sense that your sharpening service will be successful, there's absolutely no harm in starting with a higher-end Wicked Edge sharpener right from the start. It will save you time in sharpening each knife. If you already own or work for a business and are looking to bring in knife sharpening as an additional source of revenue, and you have the funds to purchase a higher-end model, then I recommend doing that because you'll reduce your labor cost on each knife.

If you would like to purchase a high-end Wicked Edge sharpener, the specific model to purchase will depend on the type of sharpening service you plan to operate. If the vast majority of the knives you plan to sharpen will be kitchen knives, choose the Generation 3 Pro–this is what I use. It's extremely fast and convenient to operate. If you plan to sharpen a variety of different knife types, like kitchen knives, pocketknives, hunting and fishing knives, and so on, choose the Precision Sharpener WE130. It lacks a little bit of the convenience compared to the Generation 3 Pro, but it has a wider range of angle settings and more adjustability, making it more versatile and better suited for more diverse sharpening services.

CHOOSING YOUR SHARPENING ABRASIVES

The primary abrasives available for Wicked Edge sharpening systems are diamond sharpening stones. Diamond stones are extremely hard, and they very aggressively remove material from a blade, though not nearly as fast as an electric sharpening system. They can remove material from any knife, regardless of how hard the blade material may be. Blades made from softer steels are easy to remove material from. You'll find it more time-consuming to remove material from harder, higher-quality steels, but you can achieve excellent results regardless of the steel hardness. For each grit size of abrasive included with each Wicked Edge sharpener, two of each grit are provided so you can sharpen both sides of the knife simultaneously. The sharpening stones are mounted to a handle, which has a precisely fitted hole through the center so the handle can slide on the sharpener's guide rods, which hold the angle while you sharpen the knife.

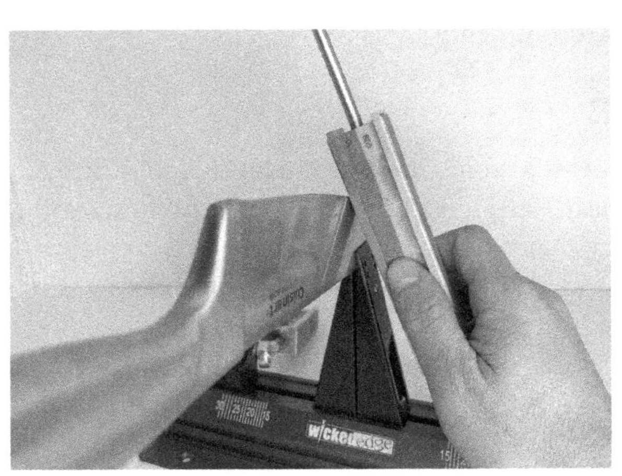

When using abrasives to remove material from an edge, the abrasives create scratches in the edge where the material is removed. Coarse stones, like 100 grit, are necessary to remove material from an edge quickly, but they create larger, deep scratches and produce an edge that isn't very sharp. Fine stones create sharp edges, but only after deeper scratches from coarser abrasives are removed fist. Fine stones will not remove deep scratches without a lot of work. So the best results are achieved the most quickly by progressing through a series of abrasives that begin with a coarse stone, progress through several medium grit stones, and then finish with a fine stone. This series is called an abrasive progression, or **grit progression**.

To have the ability to remove metal quickly, and refine an edge to a level of sharpness that will truly impress your customers, these are the grits of diamond stones you'll need: 100, 200, 400, 600, 800, and 1,000 grit. These are the exact abrasives I use on 98 percent of the knives I sharpen for my customers. Regardless of the types of knives you're sharpening and the types of customers you develop, the prior mentioned assortment of abrasives will be the minimum assortment required for you to be successful. My sharpening service is focused primarily on kitchen knives for households, so the 100- to 1,000-grit stone assortment is really all I use.

Though the 100- to 1,000-grit diamond stone assortment will please just about any customer, there are other types of abrasives that you can use to produce different edge finishes, which may be useful if you plan to sharpen knives for customers outside of the home-cooking market. These are the other abrasive options available for Wicked Edge knife-sharpening systems that I recommend:

CERAMIC STONES

Ceramic sharpening stones are softer than diamond stones, which means they are not nearly as aggressive. They are useful for creating more refined edges with tiny micro teeth. Ceramic stones are frequently used to follow diamond stones in grit progression to polish edges and create a shinier look. Ceramic stones are also commonly used for touching up knives that are already in good condition and don't require a lot of material removal.

LEATHER STROPS

Leather, when used as a sharpening medium, is very effective for cleaning up and polishing edges after harder mediums, like diamond or ceramic stones, are used. Leather strops are often paired with stropping compounds, like diamond emulsion or diamond paste, which should be applied to the leather strop. Leather has what's called a burnishing effect on an edge, which means it smears the molecules around and pulls them closer together, which smooths the edge. Leather strops remove all micro teeth and produce a very fine edge. This type of edge is most useful for shaving, which is why leather strops are used by barbers to sharpen straight razors. They are also useful to create a highly polished edge on a regular knife.

DIAMOND LAPPING FILM

Lapping film is a polyester plastic impregnated with diamond particles. It has an adhesive backing, and usually comes on sheets of multiple strips. Lapping film is incredible at polishing edges, and I highly recommend using it if your goal is to achieve a mirror edge for your customers. To use it, Wicked Edge offers handles for their sharpeners that have a blank piece of glass. Simply peel the Lapping film strip off the sheet and stick it to the glass, and then use it like you would any other Wicked Edge sharpening stone.

ABRASIVE COMBINATIONS FOR DIFFERENT MARKET SEGMENTS

These are the abrasive combinations I recommend for each market segment:

Home cooks

- Diamond stones: 100, 200, 400, 600, 800, and 1,000 grit

Professional chefs

- Diamond stones: 100, 200, 400, 600, 800, 1,000, 1,500, and 2,200 grit
- Ceramic stones: Wicked Edge Micro Fine Ceramic Stones Pack (1.4/0.6 micron)

Everyday pocketknife users

- Diamond stones: 100, 200, 400, 600, 800, and 1,000 grit

Hunters

- Diamond stones: 100, 200, 400, 600, 800, and 1,000 grit
- Leather strops: 5 and 3.5 micron

Fishermen

- Diamond stones: 100, 200, 400, 600, 800, and 1,000 grit

Military/law enforcement/tactical

- Diamond stones: 100, 200, 400, 600, 800, 1,000, 1,500, and 2,200 grit

Fire/rescue/EMS

- Diamond stones: 100, 200, 400, 600, 800, and 1,000 grit

High-end knife collectors

- Diamond Stones: 100, 200, 400, 600, 800, 1,000, 1,500, 2,200, and 3,000 grit
- Diamond Lapping Film: 9, 6, and 3 microns (remember to purchase the Wicked Edge product for mounting and using lapping film, which is called the Blank Handles and Glass Platens Pack)
- Leather strops with 4-, 2-, 1-, and 0.5-micron diamond emulsion

Specialty Sharpening

Knives are the most common tools that need sharpening, but you may consider offering sharpening services for different types of tools as your business grows. These are the other common tools for which there is a high demand for sharpening:

- scissors
- hair-cutting shears
- axes and hatchets
- garden shears
- saw blades
- chisels
- plane blades
- lawn mower blades

All the blade types listed above will require unique sharpening tools or equipment. Wicked Edge offers an attachment for scissors and an attachment for chisels and plane blades. Though it's not necessary to get your business started, purchasing more sharpening equipment will help you expand and grow your sharpening service. Once you've expanded your sharpening service to offer sharpening for more blade types, you can set a unique price for each of the different types of blades that you sharpen, depending on the equipment you use and how much time it takes to sharpen each blade type.

EVERYTHING YOU'LL NEED TO GET STARTED

When launching you knife-sharpening business, I recommend starting out with the minimum number of items needed to start making money. Once you start making money, use your profits to purchase additional equipment–if you think it's necessary for the type of sharpening service you are offering. This list includes everything you'll need to get started:

- portable Wicked Edge knife sharpener
- diamond sharpening stones in 100, 200, 400, 600, 800, and 1,000 grit
- spray bottle
- rubbing alcohol (91 percent is better, but 70 percent works too)
- black permanent markers
- paper towels
- thin leather cut to one-inch-by-one-inch strips, or a roll of mole-skin—for knife clamping
- a minimum of five plastic bins for knife storage (optimum size is fourteen inches by eleven inches by three inches)
- dish towels to use as liners for each of your plastic bins
- ten to twenty inexpensive knives to practice learning how to use the sharpener
- one or two pairs of cut-proof gloves

Total cost for all the items on the above list: **approximately $500 to $600** if you choose a low-end, portable Wicked Edge sharpener. If you choose a high-end Wicked Edge sharpener and decide to purchase more sharpening abrasives and accessories, expect your start-up cost to range from $1,000 to $1,300.

The above list is exactly what I used when I started my business. I later added a higher-end Wicked Edge sharpener model called the Generation 3 Pro Sharpener (cost $899) to reduce my sharpening time per knife, but the other items on the list remain the same, and I use them daily. The purpose of some of the more miscellaneous items on this list will be discussed in detail in the next chapter.

If you plan to sharpen knives at locations other than your home, you may also need a portable table and chair. When shopping for a portable table, try to find the sturdiest one possible. Test to see if it rocks from side to side with little effort. If it does, it's no good. When you acquire your table, it's helpful to drill two holes in it that match the mounting holes on the portable Wicked Edge sharpener. Use some long bolts and wingnuts to attach the sharpener to the table, so it can be easily removed when it's time to pack up.

CHAPTER 8

SHARPENING FUNDAMENTALS

Wicked Edge sharpening systems are unique. As previously stated, there are many good angle-guided sharpening systems on the market, but none except Wicked Edge allow you to sharpen both sides of the blade simultaneously. Wicked Edge sharpeners work by clamping the blade with the edge facing upward in a vise. With the blade clamped in this position, both of your hands are free to sharpen.

With both of your hands working on the knife, the sharpener needs to be stabilized so it doesn't move around while you sharpen. Some Wicked Edge models are designed to be C-clamped to a table, others can be mounted to a heavy base, and the larger models are heavy enough to stand freely on their own.

Once the blade is clamped in a Wicked Edge sharpener, the angle can be adjusted on both sides of the sharpener. Some Wicked Edge sharpener models allow you to adjust each side individually and allow for asymmetric sharpening angles. Other Wicked Edge sharpener models are designed for speed and convenience and allow you to adjust the angle on both sides of the knife simultaneously with the pull of a single lever. Every Wicked Edge sharpening system has incremental angle adjustment settings in increments of one degree or less, allowing you to match the angle of the edge very precisely. There is no play in any of the components, so once the sharpening angle is locked in, the abrasive will contact the knife at the exact same angle with every stroke.

With the knife mounted in the sharpener, the angle adjustments locked in place, and the sharpening stones mounted onto the sharpener, all that's left for you to do is push the sharpening stones against the knife's edge. The one factor that complicates the sharpening process is the knife. Knives come in many different shapes and sizes, so the learning curve you must overcome is how to recognize which actions to take based on the observations you make about each knife.

DETERMINING A KNIFE'S SHARPENING ANGLE

Using a Wicked Edge or any other precise angle-guided sharpening system to find the correct sharpening angle for a knife is incredibly easy. All you need is visibility and to do some trial and error with the sharpener's angle settings. For visibility, color the knife's edge with a black marker. The purpose of this is so you can see where in the edge the coloring is removed when a stone contacts the edge. Use a fine abrasive, like 600 grit or higher, and test some different sharpening angles until you find an angle that allows the abrasive to remove the coloring from the entire edge of the knife. When you find that angle, you can lock in your angle settings on the sharpener.

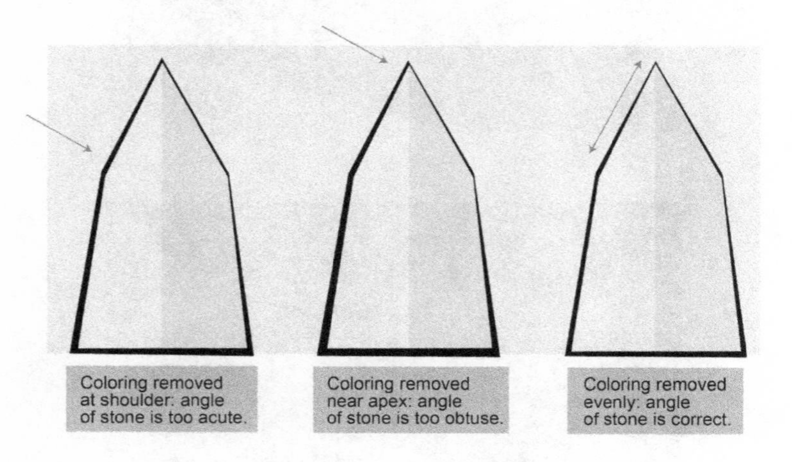

You'll most likely be able to see where the coloring is removed with your naked eye. If it's difficult for you to see, use a magnifying glass. It's very helpful in either case to have good lighting.

Out of everything about how to sharpen knives in this book, this is the most important piece of advice I can give: **Let the knife tell you what angle to use for sharpening**. Do not choose the angle yourself or let anyone else, including the manufacturer of the knife, tell you the angle. Knife manufacturers often sharpen knives without precise angle control, using electric sharpening equipment because it is fast and efficient. Though they have an idea of what the edge angle should be, in my experience, the edge angle I find on knives is usually different from the sharpening angle that is recommended by the manufacturer on their website. This discrepancy could also be from prior, unprofessional sharpening jobs that altered the edge angle. Because of these factors, there's simply no way to be sure of the angle unless you discover it for yourself. When you or someone else chooses the angle for the knife, instead of letting the knife tell you the angle, you'll almost always remove too much material, and you'll spend entirely way too much time sharpening to remove that unnecessary amount of material. Use a marker to color the edge for visibility. Perform trial and error with different angle settings until the coloring is removed evenly. It's that simple, and you'll produce much better results in significantly less time.

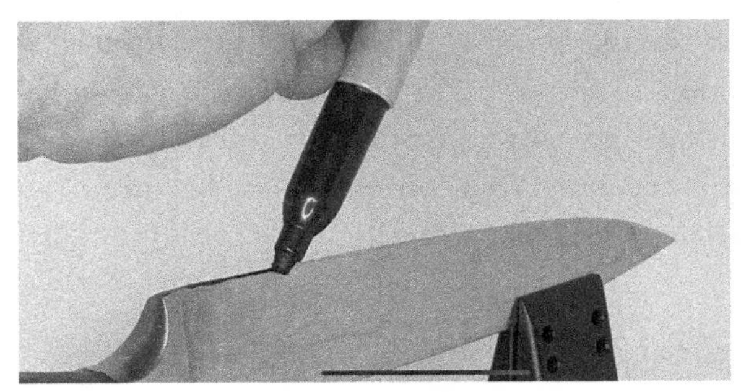

In addition to saving you time in sharpening and allowing you to remove a minimal amount of material from the knife, matching the existing edge angle will also help you from altering the appearance of the blade. Owners of expensive cutlery can be very particular about the aesthetics of their knives. If you use an incorrect sharpening angle, you could accidentally permanently alter the appearance of the knife, angering your customer and hurting your reputation. Most of the time, irreparable damage that changes the appearance of the knife happens when you use a sharpening angle that is *too acute* and remove material from the shoulder of the edge. When you do this, the bevel will widen, which many knife owners don't find aesthetically pleasing.

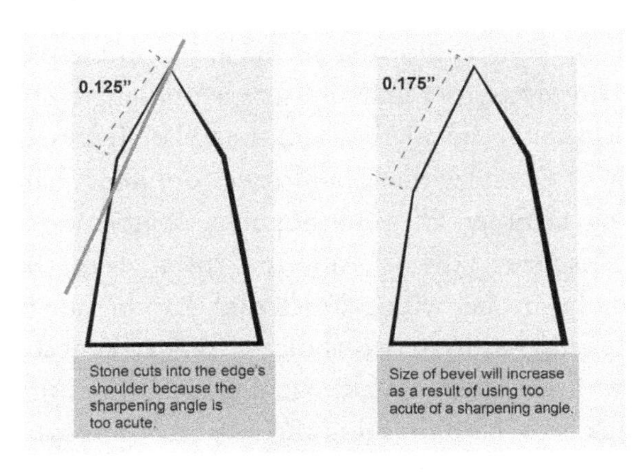

If you were wondering at the beginning of the last chapter why you wouldn't sharpen all knives at a more acute sharpening angle to produce sharper results, this is why. This and the unnecessary time you'll spend sharpening when using an angle that's too acute. It's for these reasons that I will start with a wider sharpening angle, like 25-plus degrees per side, if I am not 100 percent sure about the sharpening angle after performing trial and error with the marker. Though acute angles produce sharper knives, wider angles are a lot more cautious. Caution is a good thing, especially when working with knives that cost hundreds of dollars each. As a professional knife sharpener, it's your job to find the balance between achieving maximum sharpness and using caution to protect your customer's knives.

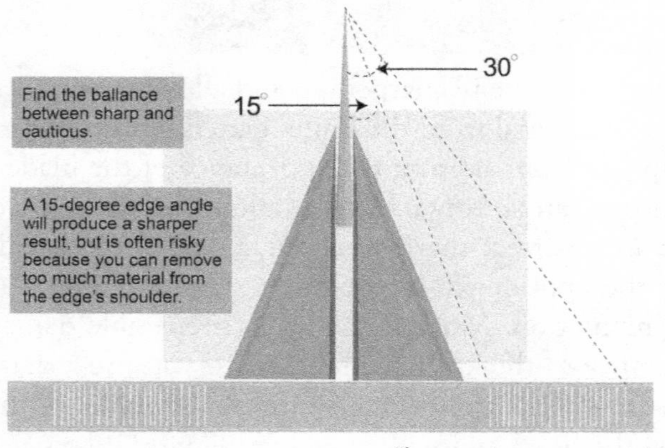

I have seen countless people make the mistake of assuming that the angle on one side of the knife is the same as the angle on the other side of the knife, so they simply test to find the sharpening angle on one side and don't repeat this test on the other side of the knife. This is a huge mistake. There are a lot of variables that could cause different sharpening angles from one side to the other, like prior unguided sharpening jobs, or simply how the knife was made. Always test to find the angle on both sides of the knife before you begin sharpening. You'll find that they are often different. If they are different, you have two choices. You can choose to change the angle on one or both sides to make them even. Choosing to change the angle of an edge is called reprofiling the edge. Or you can leave them as you found them and sharpen them asymmetrically. Some people believe edge angles need to be symmetrical from one side of the knife to the other to achieve sharpness. That's simply not true. Sharpness is determined by the inclusive angle of the edge. It is true that a 40-degree inclusive edge is sharper than a 50-degree inclusive edge. However, the inclusive edge of 18 degrees on one side of the knife and 22 degrees on the other side of the knife is the exact same as 20 degrees on both sides of the knife. Both scenarios equal a 40-degree inclusive edge angle.

If you do choose to reprofile the knife to make a symmetrical edge, I highly recommend sharpening each side to match the *wider* angle. For instance, if you find the edge on the left is 23 degrees, and the edge on the right is 20 degrees, make them both 23 degrees. If you choose to make them both 20 degrees, you'll remove metal from the edge at the shoulder on the side that is 23 degrees, which will widen the bevel on that side of the knife only. Reprofiling to the angle of the more obtuse side is also much less time consuming than reprofiling to the angle of the more acute side of the knife.

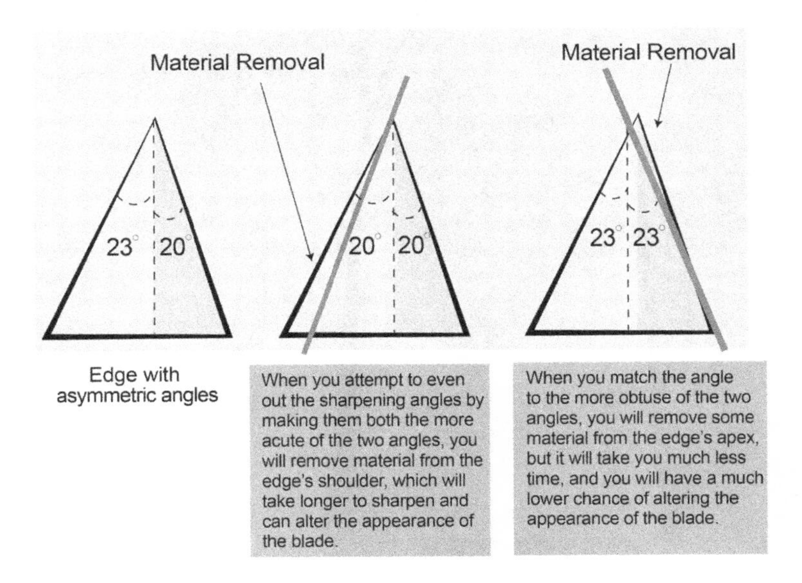

The majority of knife owners will not notice a difference in the performance of an edge that is 46 degrees inclusive vs. 40 degrees inclusive. It's in your favor to choose the wider of the two angles as your sharpening angle because you'll save a lot of time sharpening, and there is a much lower chance of damaging the knife.

IDENTIFYING EDGE GRINDS

There are key indicators that you can look out for when using the marker method to find the edge angle that will alert you to different edge grinds. Wicked Edge sharpening equipment produces V grinds. When you come across a knife with a convex grind, you'll need to convert it to a V grind.

If the coloring from the marker is removed in the center of the edge, but not the top or bottom of the edge, it means you've discovered a convex or rounded edge. It takes a fair amount of work to convert a convex grind to a V grind. It's not difficult to figure out–it just takes a little patience.

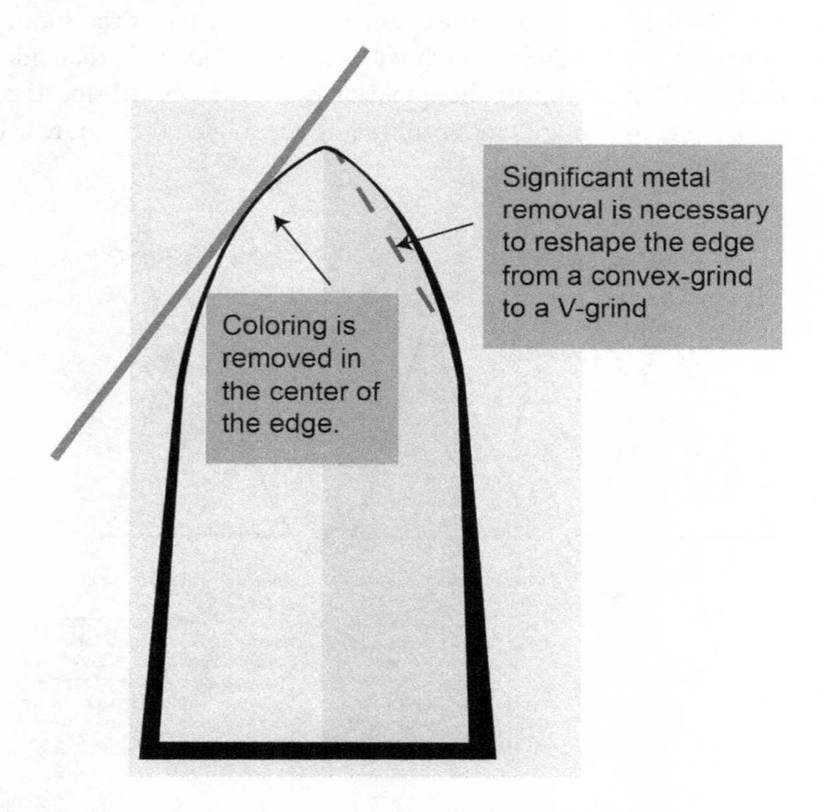

To recap: When preparing to sharpen a knife, always remember to examine the knife before you begin sharpening. Determine the proper edge angle by using the marker method, and never make assumptions or let anyone tell you about what sharpening angle to use on the knife. Your first priority should be to protect the knife and prevent damage to it, and your second priority should be to make the knife as sharp as possible.

ANGLE CALIBRATIONS AND SHARPENING GEOMETRY

All Wicked Edge sharpener models are calibrated for when the edge of the knife rests five-eighths of one inch above the top of the vise. The angle changes as the clamping height is increased or decreased from that height. What this means is if you clamp a knife so the edge rests one inch over the top of the vise, and you set your sharpening angle to 20 degrees, your actual sharpening angle will be closer to 19 degrees. Increasing the height lowers the angle, and decreasing the height widens the sharpening angle.

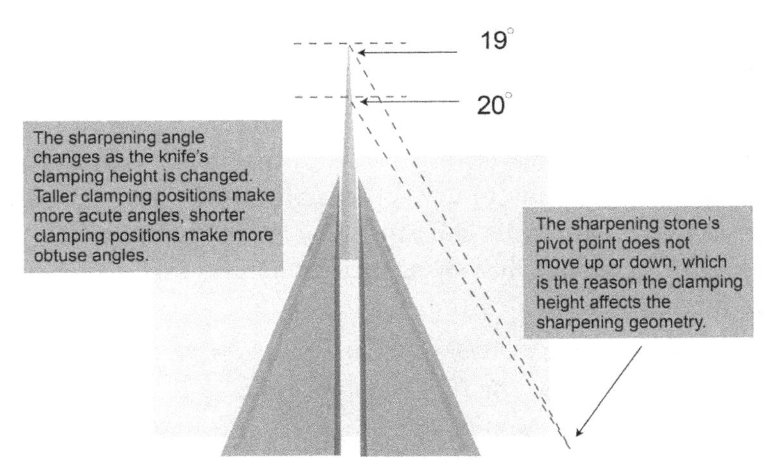

It's important for you to know this so you understand how the sharpener works, and just as important to shove it to the back of your mind and not think about it. If you used the marker method to find the sharpening angle and determined the 20-degree mark on the sharpener is the correct angle for the knife, do you care if the actual sharpening angle is 19 degrees? I'll answer for you. You do not, and neither will the vast majority of your customers who just want a sharp knife to cut their vegetables and don't care about anything else. The marker does not lie. If the coloring comes off evenly from the edge when the sharpening angle is set to the 20-degree mark on the sharpener, you know the correct angle for the knife, regardless of what that actual angle may be. Don't get caught up in the math or you'll make yourself crazy and probably ruin some knives in the process. Trust the marker and let the rest of the math go. The difference in the performance of the edge between 19 and 20 degrees is so nominal that no one will ever know or care about the difference when using the knife.

The reason it's important for you to know this is because changing the knife height gives you an extra variable you can manipulate to achieve the correct angle for a knife. For instance, if you are trying to sharpen a German-style chef's knife and find that you've maxed out the sharpener's angle settings to 30 degrees per side and still can't remove the coloring from the apex of the edge, you can lower the knife in the clamp to squeeze a little wider of an angle out of the sharpener. The same is true in the opposite direction. If you need to achieve a slightly more acute angle than the sharpener's angle settings will allow to match the existing angle of a knife's edge, you can raise up the knife in the clamp to make the sharpening angle more acute.

The only exception to not providing perfection with angles is if you're operating a sharpening service that caters to customers with very specific demands. If you're looking to develop customers who are very particular about their knives, like knife collectors, you'll need to know how to provide a sharpening service that meets their demands. This is an example of a request I received from a customer:

> *"I would like to have my Chris Reeves Sebenza pocketknife sharpened to a mirror finish at exactly 17.5 degrees per side."*

As previously discussed, the size of the knife and the clamping height will impact the sharpening geometry, so the angle markings on the Wicked Edge sharpener aren't 100 percent accurate all the time. To meet a request like this from a customer, you must use a Digital Angle Gauge. If you're not familiar with what this is, it's a digital tool that provides exact angle measurements. All you need to do is zero the gauge on the sharpener and then hold it to your sharpening stone, then tilt the sharpening stone so it contacts the knife's edge. Once it makes contact, the gauge will provide you with a digital readout of the current angle of the sharpening stones. With this information, you can adjust the angle settings as necessary to achieve the angle you want with incredible accuracy.

However, even if the customer makes a very specific request for a sharpening angle, **do not start sharpening the customer's knife until you've performed the marker test first**. It's likely the customer doesn't know what the actual angle of the knife's edge is, and you must assume they don't. Requests like this happen when customers receive a recommendation about how the knife should be sharpened, usually from the manufacturer or another source online. Because you don't know the validity of the recommendation, you must do your due diligence and test the knife's edge for the current angle before you proceed. If the actual angle of the knife is 25 degrees per side, and the customer requests 17.5 degrees per side, not only will it take you an hour to sharpen, there is a strong likelihood that you'll completely alter the appearance of the knife. Always use the marker method to check what the angle is first, then decide about how to proceed from there. If the knife's edge angle is within two degrees of the customer's request, I go ahead and sharpen the knife as requested. If it's any more than two degrees different, I will contact the customer and ask how he or she would like to proceed, and I make sure to tell the customer that sharpening at the requested angle will change the appearance of the knife permanently. Some customers will be okay with that, and others will tell you to sharpen the knife so it keeps the factory appearance.

CHAPTER 9

LEARNING TO USE A WICKED EDGE SHARPENER

On my first day working for Wicked Edge in February 2012, Clay handed me a box of about fifteen cheap kitchen knives to sharpen. He showed me how to clamp a knife in the sharpener and how to adjust the angle settings. He then colored in the edge of the first knife with a marker, told me to set the sharpening angle to 20 degrees on both sides of the knife, sharpen with the coarsest stone until all the coloring was removed from the edge on both sides, and make 100 passes with each of the other five grits of sharpening stones that were laid out in front of me, progressing from the coarsest stone to the finest. Once I was done, he instructed me to repeat the same process on all the knives in the box. His intention was for me to get a feel for how the sharpener worked and to help me develop the muscle memory to use the sharpener comfortably. It took me nearly four hours to sharpen all of the knives, but when I was done, I felt confident in my ability to produce incredibly sharp edges, and I felt comfortable using the sharpener.

Your first step to learning how to use your sharpening equipment is to acquire ten to twenty knives to practice on. Try to find a decent variety of knife types, like chef's knives, fillet knives, utility knives, paring knives, steak knives, pocketknives, and so on. Goodwill or other secondhand goods stores sell knives very inexpensively, and you can usually find knives for sale at flea markets for less than five dollars each.

There are three main processes to using a Wicked Edge knife sharpener: clamping the knife, setting the angle, and sharpening the knife. Though these steps sound quite simple, there's actually a lot involved in performing each step. Wicked Edge offers an awesome assortment of tutorials on their website and on YouTube. A detailed instruction manual is also included with every sharpener. The details about using the sharpening equipment discussed in this chapter will provide you with a basic understanding of how the equipment works, but mainly the purpose of the instructions in this chapter is to provide you with the tricks I've learned over the years that will help shorten your learning curve and make sharpening easier for you.

When you first begin using a Wicked Edge sharpener, it's important to know that Wicked Edge diamond stones have a break-in period. During the manufacturing process diamond particles get stuck to each other on the surface of the plates and form a second layer of particles on top of the base layer. What this means is the stones will be extremely aggressive when you first start using them. They will feel gritty and make a terrible grinding sound before they are broken in. Fortunately, it only takes about fifteen knives to break in the stones, which is about the same number of knives you need to practice on to develop your technique.

Once the diamond stones are broken in, they'll continue to get smoother and smoother, which produces better results. They will continue to produce finer, sharper results until they eventually wear out. The number of knives that can be sharpened before the stones wear out depends on several factors:

- the amount of pressure you apply with the stones against the knife
- the hardness of the steel being sharpened
- the number of strokes you perform with each stone on each knife

There's not much you can do about the hardness of the steel you sharpen—that's up to your customers. But you do have control over the other two factors. To keep your stones in great condition for a long time, use less pressure and try not to exceed twenty strokes with each stone on each side of the knife. There are times when you'll need to perform more strokes, like when you are reprofiling a knife's edge or attempting to create a highly polished edge, but try to limit the number of strokes you make because it will extend the life of your stones and take you less time to sharpen each knife.

You don't need to use a lot of pressure with the stones. I use a fair amount of pressure with my coarse stone when I first start the sharpening process to reshape the edge, and then I use very light pressure with the rest of my stones. Using less pressure will not only help keep your stones in great shape, but you'll also produce sharper knives.

Wicked Edge diamond stones occasionally need to be cleaned because they get clogged up with metal shavings that come off knives as you sharpen. I usually clean my stones after I've sharpened about fifty knives. You can clean Wicked Edge diamond stones under running water with a soft toothbrush. Then dry them with a paper towel and stand them on their ends to allow them to completely dry overnight. If you have Wicked Edge ceramic stones, *do not* get them wet. If you do, the adhesive that holds them to the plastic Wicked Edge stone handles will fail, and the stones will come loose from the handles. Ceramic stones should be cleaned with a Superaser or household eraser.

All Wicked Edge stones should always be used dry. Do not apply sharpening oil or water to them. If you do, the water or oil will catch metal shavings as they're coming off the knife, and the stones will clog up very quickly. Always use the stones dry so they can perform well and work quickly.

KNIFE CLAMPING

Clamping a knife in any Wicked Edge sharpener is easy to do. Wicked Edge knife clamps are made from aluminum. The jaws have an anodized finish, which helps prevent the jaws from scratching knives. Knife steel is harder than aluminum, so the chances of the jaws scratching the knife are low, but not zero. If the knife moves in the clamp while sharpening, it could get scratched. For this reason, I highly recommend always putting something soft in the jaws or wrapped around the knife to prevent scratching. My favorite material to wrap around the knife for clamping is thin leather. The other material I use very frequently is moleskin, which is a medical product designed to put in shoes to prevent and ease the pain from blisters. Moleskin has an adhesive backing, so instead of wrapping it around the spine of the knife, you can simply cut two slivers of it and stick them to the inside of the sharpener's jaws.

There are four benefits to inserting leather or moleskin in the sharpener's vise:

- prevents scratching
- helps the vise grip the knife better so it doesn't move up or down while sharpening

- prevents the knife from rocking from side to side during sharpening
- reduces strain on the sharpener's vise

Many kitchen knives are what the knife industry calls "fully flat ground." For example, the vast majority of eight-inch chef's knives are fully flat ground. This means the spine of the knife tapers all the way to the edge of the knife. These knives will want to rock from side to side in the sharpener's vise as you sharpen and can be difficult to clamp so they stay upright. This is especially true for Wicked Edge sharpeners that have Wicked Edge's standard vise, like the Wicked Edge GO. The two inside faces of the vise are parallel to each other. When a triangle shape, which is what a fully-flat-ground blade is, is wedged between two parallel faces, the triangle will try to tilt to one side as the parallel faces are tightened together.

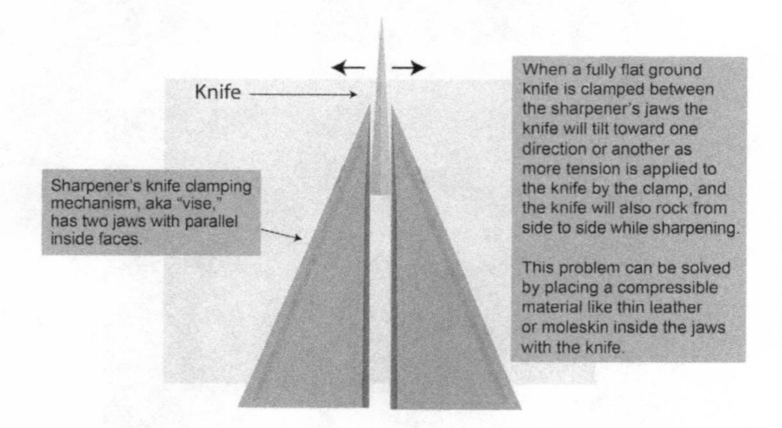

When thin leather or moleskin is inserted in the vise with the knife, it will compress at the knife's thickest point as the vise is tightened. It will stay less compressed along the thinner area of the knife where there is less clamping pressure, which fills the gap between the knife and the jaws to keep the knife upright and prevents it from rocking from side to side during sharpening.

Inserting leather or moleskin in the sharpener's vise also helps prevent strain on the sharpening equipment. When an aluminum jaw contacts a steel knife blade and is tightened together by bolts that are also made of steel, the result will be a fair amount of strain on the aluminum jaws.

Wicked Edge sharpeners are very well built from aircraft-grade aluminum, but they are tools, and all tools can eventually break. By inserting leather or moleskin inside the sharpener's vise when clamping a knife, a lot of that pressure is absorbed by the leather or moleskin, which relieves some of the strain on the aluminum parts. This helps the sharpener stay in great condition for a much longer timeframe.

If thin leather or moleskin is not available to you, fold up a paper towel four times, and then cut a one-inch-by-one-inch section of it to wrap around the knife for clamping. I have seen many, many people tape up their knives with painter's tape or masking tape to help prevent the jaws from scratching the knife. I don't recommend this solution. I find taping the knife causes the knife to want to move in the sharpener's vise during sharpening because of the slick outside surface of the tape and the low adhesive quality of painter's tape and masking tape. By my own comparison on hundreds of knives, I have found that using something with more cushion, like leather, moleskin, or several layers of paper towel, is a much more favorable solution.

In addition to using leather or moleskin to help prevent strain on the sharpening equipment, it's also very important to be mindful of how hard you tighten the vise to clamp a knife. You don't need to use a lot of pressure. Don't force the bolts to tighten more when they already feel very tight. You're simply clamping a knife, not tightening the lug nuts on a tire.

SETTING THE SHARPENING ANGLE

As previously discussed, using a marker to determine the right sharpening angle for a knife is the best solution. Knife manufacturers' recommendations are often not completely accurate. Knives can be sharpened by many sharpening solutions before making it into your hands, which may have altered the edge geometry. This is the procedure for using a marker to determine the correct sharpening angle for a knife:

1. Color the knife's edge, on both sides, with a black marker. The easiest way to do this is to stab the marker onto the knife's edge at the back of the knife, and then run it all the way down to the tip of the knife.

2. Use a fine stone (600 grit or higher) and make a pass with the stone against the knife's edge.
3. Look to see where the marker is removed on one side of the knife.
    a. If the coloring is removed at the shoulder of the edge and not the middle or top of the edge, the angle is too acute. Widen the sharpening angle and try again.
    b. If the coloring is removed at the top of the edge and not the middle or the shoulder of the edge, the angle is too wide. Decrease the sharpening angle and try again.
    c. When you find a sharpening angle that allows the stone to remove the majority of the coloring from the whole edge, from the shoulder to the edge's apex, that is the correct sharpening angle for the knife.
4. Repeat step 1 through 3 on the other side of the knife.

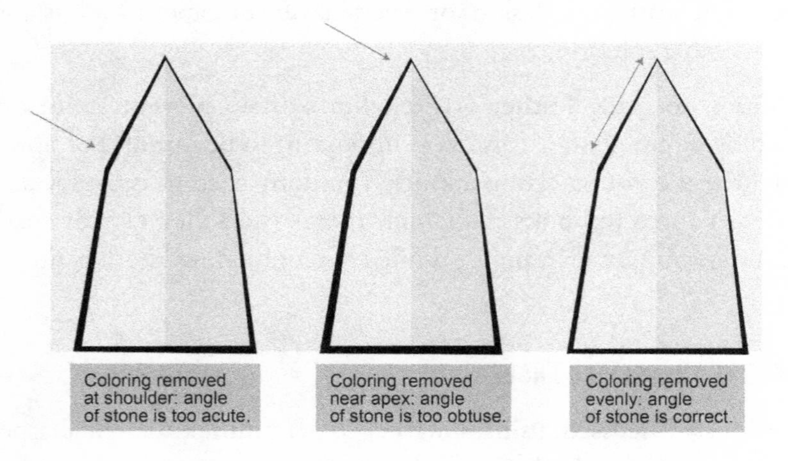

It can sometimes be difficult to see where the coloring is removed from the edge. Use good lighting and use a magnifying glass if you need to. Sometimes, it can be hard to determine a good sharpening angle for the knife because there is an inconsistent pattern showing where the coloring is removed. If the knife has been very poorly sharpened, you'll definitely notice areas of the knife where the marker comes off evenly from the shoulder to the top of the edge, and other areas of the knife where the marker only comes off the shoulder of the edge. When this happens, I advise finding what angle it takes to remove the marker at the part of the edge where it didn't come off the edge's apex. That angle will be wider than the angle of the rest of the edge. It's up to you how to proceed, but I recommend choosing the widest angle you find at any point on the knife as your sharpening angle. Wider angles are more cautions, and caution is a good thing.

If the edge is very badly rounded, it can also be difficult to find the correct sharpening angle. In this scenario, when the stone contacts the knife as you're trying different angles, you'll notice a very thin line of color is removed from the center of the edge. When you notice this, try to find an angle that allows the stone to take the coloring off near the apex of the edge. This will most likely be a wider angle, like 25-plus degrees. Again, using a wider angle is a more cautious and good decision. Use the wider angle that takes the coloring off at the top of the edge and start sharpening to remove material from the edge until all the coloring is gone.

For most people, the process of finding the correct sharpening angle for a knife using the marker trick is the most confusing and hardest to learn part of the whole sharpening process. You must practice to fully learn and understand it. When you first start using your sharpener, practice this step a lot. Try to find the correct sharpening angle for all of your practice knives. This is a procedure that you can use that will help you learn:

1. Clamp a knife in the sharpener.
2. Color the edge with a marker.
3. Set the sharpening angle to 15 degrees per side.
4. Make five light passes with your 600-grit diamond stone on each side of the knife.
5. Look to see where the marker is removed.
6. Recolor the edge with the marker, set the angle to 20 degrees per side, and repeat steps 4 and 5.
7. Recolor the edge with the marker, set the angle to 25 degrees per side, and repeat steps 4 and 5.
8. Recolor the edge with the marker, set the angle to 30 degrees per side, and repeat steps 4 and 5.
9. Repeat steps 1 through 8 on five different knives.

This process is tedious and boring, but it will greatly reduce your learning curve by showing you what to look for and how to make angle adjustments to find the correct sharpening angle for knives.

SHARPENING THE KNIFE

When you first start using a Wicked Edge sharpener, it will most likely feel weird and awkward. Your hands need time to develop muscle memory to become comfortable with using the sharpener. Be patient, and practice until the motion feels fluid and natural. It's helpful to sharpen one side of the knife at a time until you feel comfortable with one hand. Then switch and practice with your other hand. When sharpening, it's very important to make sure the stone is flat against the edge. Pay attention to this, and don't curl the stone so only a part of it contacts the edge.

There are several different strokes you can make with the sharpening stones against the knife.

UP-AND-OUT STROKE

To perform this stroke, start with the top of the sharpening stone against the back of the knife, and move the stone forward and upward to finish the stroke when the bottom of the stone comes off the tip of the knife. This stroke is also called an edge-trailing stroke because the stone is moving away from the edge of the knife. This is the most common stroke people use, and you should practice it a lot.

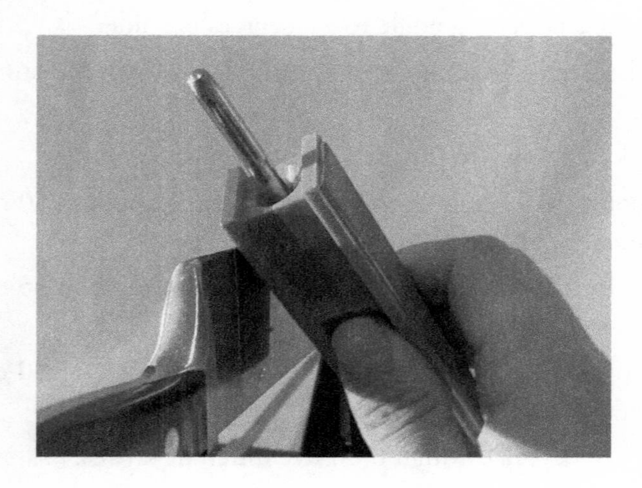

DOWN-AND-OUT STROKE

To perform this stroke, start with the bottom of the stone against the back of the knife, and move the stone forward and downward to finish the stroke when the top of the stone comes off the tip of the knife. The down-and-out stroke is also called an edge-leading stroke because the stone is moving into the edge of the knife. This stroke is useful for sharpening flexible blades.

SCRUBBING STROKE

To perform this stroke, scrub the stone against the knife moving in an up-and-down motion, with the stone never breaking contact with the edge. This stroke is very useful for removing material from an edge quickly.

SPIRAL STROKE

This stroke is just like the scrubbing stroke, only instead of moving the stone in an up-down motion, move the stone in a spiral motion with the stone never breaking contact with the edge of the knife. This stroke will also remove material quickly from the edge.

MY SHARPENING PROCESS

When I sharpen knives, I primarily use a scrubbing stroke with my coarse stone to remove material from the edge of the knife. After I am done removing material from the edge, I use an up-and-out stroke when I progress through the rest of my stones. The exception to this is when I am sharpening a flexible blade, like a fillet knife, and in that scenario I use a scrubbing stroke to remove material with my coarse stone, and then I use a down-and-out stroke to complete the grit progression.

Many people ask me which type of stroke produces the best result. In my opinion, it doesn't make a difference one way or another, especially when you are using the knife for an everyday application like cutting vegetables. Scientifically, an edge-leading stroke (down-and-out) produces a slightly better result, but the only time this result is noticeable is when measuring with a highly calibrated sharpness-testing machine. For typical use, the difference in results between the strokes is nominal.

When making strokes with the stone against the knife, it is important not to let the stone curl into the edge's tip when the stone reaches the front of the knife. The stone will naturally want to curl inward when you reach the tip of the knife. You'll feel when that starts to happen, and the trick is to not let it happen. These are some techniques you can use to prevent the stones from rounding the tip of the knife:

1. Grip the stone handles so your thumbs are applying forward pressure and your fingertips are only serving to steady the stone handle to prevent it from rolling over. Using forward pressure with your thumbs helps keep the stone traveling along the same sharpening plane as you move it forward against the knife's edge.
2. Lock your wrists and let the momentum come from your elbows and shoulders.
3. When using an up-and-out stroke or down-and-out stroke, pretend the tip of the knife is about one inch away from where it actually is, and then follow all the way through with your stroke.

DRAWING A BURR—THIS IS IMPORTANT

Drawing a burr from an edge is an incredibly important part of the sharpening process. Without performing this step, you could spend twenty minutes sharpening a knife, and when you're done, you may find that the knife did not become sharp. When anyone asks me why their knife didn't get sharp, my first question to them is always, "Did you draw a burr?" Usually, the answer is no, or they don't fully understand the concept of drawing a burr.

A burr, also called a wire edge, is a very thin strip of metal that forms along the edge of the knife once the sharpening stones contacts the apex of the edge.

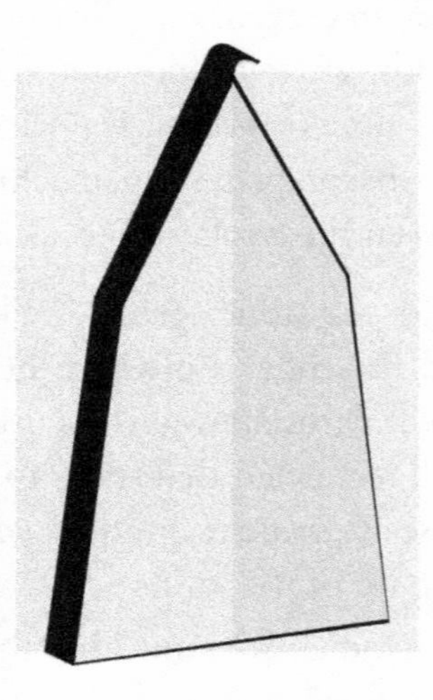

A burr is the indicator that your stones are touching the edge's apex. If the sharpening stones are not reaching the apex of the edge, a burr will not be formed, and the edge will not be sharp yet.

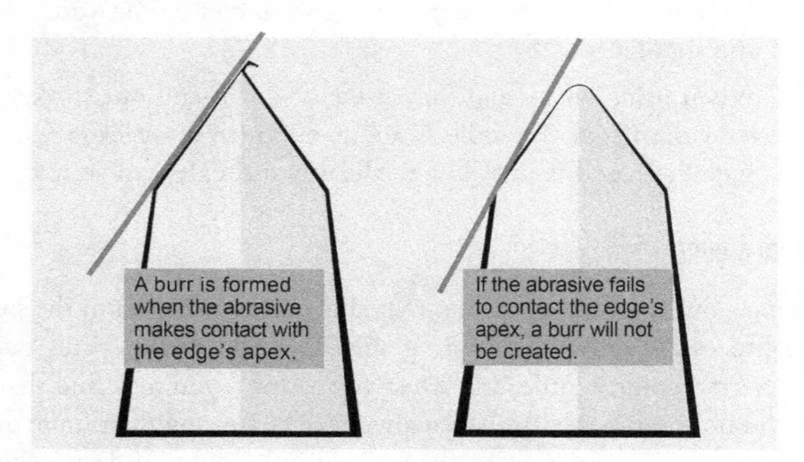

To draw a burr from a knife's edge, work on only one side of the knife with your coarse stone. You can use any stroke that you like, but I prefer a scrubbing stroke for this step. After about 30 seconds of scrubbing, check for the burr by feeling the opposite side of the edge with your finger. Run your finger up the blade toward the apex and feel for a slight snag. If you feel a snag on your finger, you've created a burr. If you do not feel a snag, you have more work to do.

If you don't feel a burr after two attempts of scrubbing for thirty seconds, it means you are probably using too acute of a sharpening angle for the knife. Widen your angle by 2 degrees, scrub for thirty more seconds, and try to feel for the burr again. For example, if you don't feel a burr at 20 degrees after thirty to sixty seconds of scrubbing, widen your angle to 22 degrees, scrub for thirty more seconds, and then feel for the burr again.

You must make sure there is a burr present along the entire edge of the knife. If you feel a burr in some areas but not others, scrub your stones against the edge where there is no burr yet, and check for the burr periodically until it is formed.

Once you find the burr along the whole edge of the knife on one side, you must perform the same process on the other side of the knife. Just because the stone is reaching the apex of the edge on one side, that doesn't mean the stone will reach the apex on the other side of the knife.

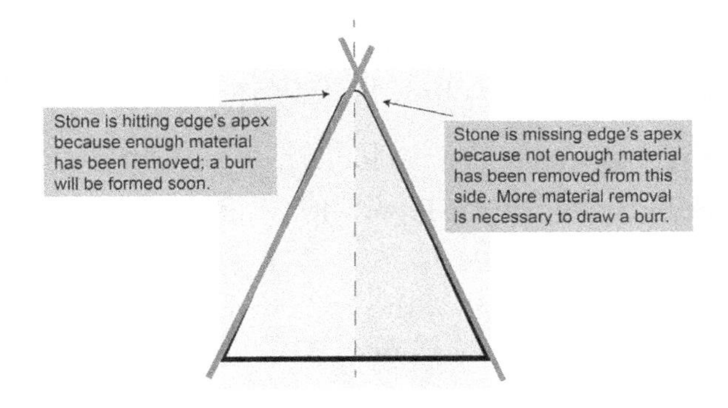

Burrs can be difficult to feel, especially to untrained hands. Smaller, less predominant burrs are formed when using lower sharpening angles, and bigger burrs that are easier to feel are formed when using wider sharpening angles. To learn what a burr feels like, you need to practice. Clamp one of your practice knives in the sharpener and set the angle to *30 degrees.* At a sharpening angle of 30 degrees, you'll almost certainly create a burr quickly. Scrub one side of the knife for sixty seconds, and then feel for the burr on the opposite side of the edge. When you feel it, make a mental note of what it feels like. Do this as many times and on as many knives as you need to until you get used to feeling for and finding the burr.

STROKE COUNT

When starting with your coarse stone, you need to perform as many strokes as necessary to remove material from the edge and draw a burr. On some knives, I will use a scrubbing motion for several minutes to restore the edge. On other knives, it takes less than twenty seconds of scrubbing to restore the edge. When reprofiling the edge of a knife made from hard steel by 5-plus degrees, it's not uncommon to need to use the coarse stone for as long as ten minutes. After the edge has been restored and a burr has been drawn from each side of the knife, I do approximately ten to twenty strokes with each stone in the grit progression on each side of the knife.

Once you've drawn the burr and have switched to your 200-grit stone, you should sharpen both sides of the blades equally by alternating your strokes from left to right with each stroke. The time it takes to complete one full stroke should be approximately one full second. To understand the momentum and timing of sharpening, say to yourself slowly in your head, *Left-side stroke, right-side stroke, left-side stroke...* The time it takes you to say, *Left-side stroke*, should take the same amount of time for the stone to travel from the back of the knife to the tip of the knife.

This is what the sharpening process looks like, step-by-step:

1. Sharpen one side of the knife with your 100-grit stone for as long as it takes to draw a burr.
2. Sharpen the other side of the knife with your 100-grit stone for as long as it takes to draw a burr.
3. Switch to your 200-grit stones.

4. Make ten to twenty strokes on each side of the knife with your 200-grit stone, alternating each stroke from left to right.
5. Repeat step 4 with your 400-grit stones.
6. Repeat step 4 with your 600-grit stones.
7. Repeat step 4 with your 800-grit stones.
8. Repeat step 4 with your 1,000-grit stones.

As you become more experienced with using the sharpener, you'll start to feel and hear when it's time to switch grits. When the stone feels like it's grabbing the knife less and you feel less resistance, and it feels more like it's gliding over the edge, that's an indicator that you can switch grits. When you start to hear a softer sound from the sharpening stones, that's because the stone is no longer grinding into the deeper scratches from the previous stone because the deeper scratches have been removed. When you hear a softer, less gritty noise, you can switch grits.

PRESSURE

When you sharpen a knife, you don't need to use a lot of pressure with the stones. In fact, the less pressure you use, the sharper the knife will get. The only time I use moderate pressure is when I am drawing a burr with my coarse stone and using a scrubbing motion. After I have drawn a burr and switched to a finer grit stone, I use very light pressure.

The motion of the stones against the knife should be very light and fluid. A mistake I commonly see people make is slapping the stones against the back of the knife when they bring their stones around for the next pass. I was terrible about doing this for many years. When you bring your stones to the back of the knife to make the next pass, very gently touch them to the knife and then start your stroke. Pay close attention to this when you're learning how to use the sharpener so you don't develop bad habits.

BE MINDFUL OF YOUR EQUIPMENT

When you operate any tool, it's important to always pay attention to how the tool is performing as you are using it, and knife-sharpening systems are no different. There are important things to watch for as you're using a Wicked Edge sharpener. Train yourself to always be mindful of these issues:

- Screws can come loose because of vibrations of abrasives while sharpening. Get in the habit of checking the tightness on thumbscrews and other threaded parts periodically while you're sharpening.
- The knife can move in the clamp. To avoid this, make sure the knife is very well secured before you begin sharpening, and avoid using too much pressure with the stones.

If at any time the knife or a screw on the sharpener moves while you are sharpening, the sharpening angle will likely change. Try to avoid this. Always check the sharpener's parts for tightness as you're sharpening. The most common reason parts come loose is the operator uses too much pressure with the stones against the knife, which causes a lot of vibration. You don't need to use a lot of pressure. In fact, you'll achieve better results if you use less pressure. If the angle does change while you are sharpening because of the knife moving or a loose screw, you may need to consider starting the sharpening process all over again, including finding the angle with the marker. If the knife moves in the clamp very briefly and not by a lot, then you can reposition it to where you had it clamped before without starting the sharpening process all over. If the knife moves significantly and you fail to notice that it moved until after you've done many strokes with the sharpening stones, you'll probably need to restart the sharpening process.

KNIFE CLEANING

During sharpening, a fair amount of metal dust will collect on the knife. There will also be some leftover coloring from the permanent marker present in small areas of the knife. You can't give knives back to your customers in this condition, so you'll need to clean the knives after you're done sharpening. The best way to clean knives is with rubbing alcohol and paper towels. I prefer to clean off knives while they're still mounted in the sharpener. It's safer to do it that way than to take the knife out and try to clean it while holding it. Spray a little bit of rubbing alcohol onto a paper towel and clean the blade by moving the paper towel upward from the spine of the knife to the edge.

SHARPENING A KNIFE FROM START TO FINISH

This is the procedure for sharpening a knife from start to finish:

Step 1: Set up your knife sharpener and your sharpening station.

- Make sure your sharpening station is clean and well organized.

Step 2: Clamp the knife in the sharpener.

- Use a thin strip of leather or moleskin when clamping the knife.

Step 3: Slide your 600-grit diamond stones onto the sharpener's guide rods.

Step 4: Use a black permanent marker to color the knife's edge on both sides.

- Stab the marker onto the edge at the back of the knife near the handle and run it all the way to the tip of the knife.

Step 5: Determine the correct sharpening angle for both sides of the knife independently by doing trial and error with some different angle settings until you find an angle that allows the stone to remove the majority of the coloring from the edge evenly from each side of the knife.

- Remember: it's okay if the angle on the left side of the sharpener does not match the angle on the right side of the sharpener.
- If you are having a hard time seeing what angle is right for the knife, choose a wider sharpening angle like 25-plus degrees per side.

Step 6: Take your 600-grit stones off the sharpener and put your 100-grit coarse stone onto the sharpener.

Step 7: Use a scrubbing motion with your 100-grit stone on one side of the knife to draw a burr.

- If you can't feel a burr after sixty seconds of scrubbing, widen your sharpening angle by 2 degrees and try again.

Step 8: Use the same process to draw a burr on the other side of the knife.

Step 9: Switch to your 200-grit stones and begin sharpening using alternating strokes.

- Make one stroke on the right side of the knife, and the next stroke on the left side of the knife. Repeat.
- You can use an up-and-out stroke, or a down-and-out stroke.

Step 10: Make ten to twenty passes on each side of the knife with each of your grits, progressing from coarse to fine.

Step 11: Check the blade for sharpness.

- Gently touch your thumbnail to the edge of the knife. If your nail catches on the knife, it's sharp. If you nail slides off the knife, it's not sharp, and you should restart the sharpening process.

Step 12: Clean off any metal dust or coloring that's left on the edge.

- Use a paper towel and rubbing alcohol.

Step 13: Remove the knife from the sharpener.

Step 14: Clean up your sharpener and sharpening station.

CHECKLIST FOR LEARNING HOW TO USE A WICKED EDGE

TASK	COMPLETE?
Acquire ten to twenty knives to practice on.	
PRACTICE YOUR STONE STROKES. • Clamp a knife in the sharpener. • Set angle to 20 degrees per side. • Color the edge on both sides with a marker. • Sharpen with your coarse stone on both sides of the knife until all the coloring is removed. • Do 100 strokes on each side of the knife with each grit, up to 1,000 grit, using a combination of different stroke techniques. • Repeat on all your practice knives.	

<table>
<tr><th>TASK</th><th>COMPLETE?</th></tr>
<tr><td>PRACTICE LEARNING HOW TO FIND THE ANGLE FOR A KNIFE USING THE MARKER METHOD.

• Clamp a knife in the sharpener.

• Color the edge with a marker.

• Make five strokes at 15, 20, 25, and 30 degrees per side with your 600-grit stone to see how the coloring is removed at each angle.

• Because you've already sharpened all your knives to 20 degrees, all the coloring should come off the edge evenly at 20 degrees. Pay attention to how that looks compared to how it looks when the coloring is removed at other angles.

• Repeat on five different knives.</td><td></td></tr>
<tr><td>PRACTICE LEARNING HOW TO FEEL FOR A BURR.

• Clamp a knife in the sharpener.

• Set the angle to 30 degrees per side.

• Scrub the edge on one side of the knife only with your coarse stone for 60 seconds.

• Practice feeling for the burr in different areas along the whole edge of the knife.

• Repeat this on five knives.</td><td></td></tr>
</table>

TASK	COMPLETE?
PRACTICE SHARPENING KNIVES FROM START TO FINISH. • Clamp a knife in the sharpener. • Use the marker method to determine the sharpening angle on both sides of the knife. • Use your coarse stone to draw a burr on one side of the knife. • Use your coarse stone to draw a burr on the other side of the knife. • Progress through your sharpening stones, alternating your strokes from left to right with every stroke, and making twenty passes with each grit on each side of the knife. • Check the edge for sharpness. • Clean off the knife using rubbing alcohol and a paper towel. • Remove the knife from the sharpener. • Repeat this on all your practice knives.	

SAFETY

When you start learning how to use a Wicked Edge, it's important to develop good safety habits. Knives will become incredibly sharp. Sharp knives are dangerous when they're not respected, and accidents can happen when people aren't paying attention. When you're handling or sharpening a knife, always keep your eyes on the knife.

The first step to staying safe while sharpening is to keep a clean workspace. When all your items are scattered, your chances of reaching for an item and accidentally brushing up against the knife in the process are much higher.

When a knife is mounted in the knife sharpener, never walk away from your sharpening station and leave the knife unattended. When a knife is mounted in a Wicked Edge sharpener, the edge faces straight up and is very exposed. If you need to leave your workstation, remove the knife from the sharpener before you get up. It would be incredibly bad to accidentally stumble when you come back to the station if a knife is mounted in the sharpener with its edge exposed.

Keep your drink away from your sharpening station. There's a lot of movement that happens when sharpening a knife. If you accidentally knock the drink over, your instinctual reaction may be to quickly reach for the drink as it's falling over. It's exactly that kind of reactional, unplanned, quick movement that you should try to avoid when working around sharp knives. I like to drink tea or hot chocolate in the evenings, but I always keep my cup on a separate table while I'm sharpening knives.

It probably goes without saying, but it's a terrible idea to sharpen knives if you have any alcohol in your system. If you've had anything to drink, don't sharpen knives. The same is true for marijuana, muscle relaxers, painkillers, or any other substance that would impair your movements and reaction time.

Never reach your arm over the knife when it's mounted in the sharpener. Reaching over an exposed knife is a sure way to get cut. To avoid this, position your sharpening stones and other items at your sharpening station so you can grab them without reaching over the knife.

Hold the stone handles by gripping them toward the bottom of the handle. If you grip the stones this way, your hands will never be above the knife where there is a danger. Pay attention to where your hands and fingers are as you are sharpening. Keep your fingers tucked in behind the stones. The most common place I cut myself is on the tip of my thumbs, which happens when I am using a scrubbing motion with the stones at the tip of the blade and the stone slips off the tip of the blade. I would have avoided this many times if I were holding the stones lower down on the handles. The other danger zone is the meat of your thumb muscle near the palm of your hand. This part of your hand is exposed when the stone comes off the tip of the knife and you bring the stone backward to make your next stroke. Be mindful of this.

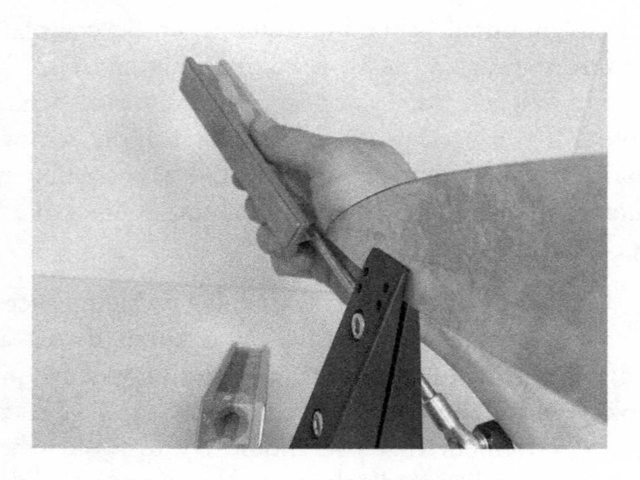

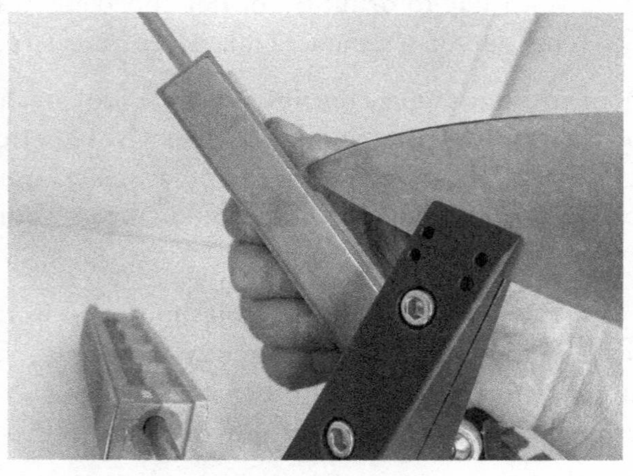

Wear cut-proof gloves. Cut-proof gloves are specifically designed to be resistant to sharp objects. There are many cut-proof glove options on the market. In my opinion, the less expensive options are not great. Spend a little more money and buy quality gloves. Wicked Edge offers cut-proof gloves made by a company called Iron Wear for twenty-five dollars per pair, and they work great. If you choose to wear cut-proof gloves, your hands will be very well protected. The downside is you'll sacrifice some dexterity in your hands and using the sharpener will be slightly more difficult.

Always keep a first-aid kit near you when sharpening. If you are sharpening at a public place, bring your first-aid kit with you. It's always better to have it and not need it than to need it and not have it. Inexpensive first-aid kits are available at almost any pharmacy. I purchased two of them for less than forty dollars total, and they include all the standard necessary items, like an assortment of Band-Aids, gauze wraps, medical tape, disinfectant wipes, and so on.

CHAPTER 10

SHARPENING SPECIFIC BLADE TYPES AND KNIFE GRINDS

NO TWO KNIVES ARE THE same, so the sharpening technique and the way you mount the knife in the sharpener will be slightly different from knife to knife. The curvature and size of each blade affects the sharpening geometry, so the way you mount the knife in the sharpener is incredibly important. There are also other factors to consider, like the flexibility of the blade and the type of edge grind.

Before you start the sharpening process on any knife, examine the knife. There are several questions you should ask yourself about the knife so you can determine the proper clamping and sharpening techniques:

- Does the edge have curvature?
- Is the blade small?
- Is the blade flexible?

OVERCOMING KNIFE CURVATURE

The curvature of the knife will determine how you should clamp it in the sharpener. Many types of kitchen knives, and most pocketknives, have curvature where the edge starts as a flat edge toward the handle, and then the edge slopes downward toward the front of the knife to form a sharp point. As a general rule, the more curvature a knife has toward the tip, the closer to the tip it should be clamped in the sharpener.

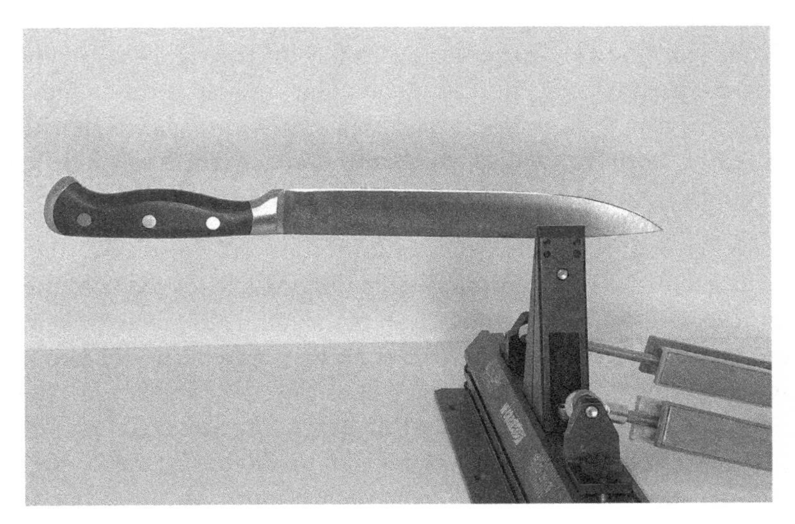

If you clamp a knife that has a lot of curvature so the clamp is positioned in the center of the blade, you'll find that as you sharpen the edge of the knife will significantly widen at the tip of the blade, and it will take a lot more time to shape the edge and draw a burr. Both of those scenarios should be avoided, and they can be easily avoided by simply clamping the knife closer to the tip.

The reason the clamping position is so important is because the sharpening geometry changes based on the curvature of the blade. If a knife with a lot of curvature is clamped farther forward, the sharpening angle will be more acute at the tip of the blade, and thus the stones will make contact with the edge's shoulder, which will cause the edge to widen. As you slide the knife backward in the clamp, the sharpening angle becomes more and more obtuse at the tip of the blade, so the stones will contact the edge at an angle that more closely matches the sharpening angle on the flat part of the edge. When a knife has a straight edge, like a Santoku knife, the sharpening geometry will not change no matter how you clamp it.

Using the marker technique will alert you if the knife is clamped too far forward or too far back. After you use the marker method to find the correct sharpening angle on the flat part of the edge, examine the edge at the tip of the knife. If you see that the coloring is removed at the shoulder of the edge, but not removed at the apex of the edge, it means the knife is clamped too far forward and you should reclamp the blade so the sharpener's vise is closer to the tip of the knife.

After you reposition the knife, recolor the edge with the marker and test it again. If you find that the coloring comes off the edge evenly, the knife position is correct. If you find that the coloring comes off at the apex of the edge, but not the shoulder, then you've gone too far. Reposition the knife slightly more forward so the clamp contacts the knife a little closer to the center.

Keep playing with the knife position until you find a position that allows the stone to remove the coloring evenly along the whole edge of the knife. This process can be tedious and time consuming, but it is well worth it because you'll save yourself a lot of time in sharpening and you'll avoid damaging a knife by widening the edge at the tip of the blade. The more experienced you become, the faster this process becomes. Fortunately, the clamping position for different types of knives can be easily predicted, and later in this chapter you'll find the optimum clamping position for many popular knife types.

ADJUSTING FOR SMALL KNIVES

Small knives require a slightly different clamping technique than regular or large-size knives. A knife that measures less than one inch from spine to edge is considered small. The issue with these knives is clearance over the top of the sharpener's vise. The edge of the knife needs to rest at least five-eighths of an inch over the top of the vise for the sharpening stones to clear the vise at lower angle settings. If the knife is clamped too low in the sharpener's vise, the sharpening stones may hit the sharpener's vise and not contact the knife's edge.

The trick to clamping small knives is to clamp them as high up in the sharpener's vise as possible. At a minimum, there should be one-eighth inch of the blade inserted into the sharpener's vise for the vise to firmly grip the knife.

When clamping blades smaller than three-quarter inches from spine to edge, it will not be possible to clamp the blade so there is one-eighth inch of blade inside the vise, and five-eighths inches of blade sticking out over the top of the vise. But increasing the clamping height is not the only thing that can be done to allow the stones to clear the vise. You can also widen the sharpening angle to get more stone clearance. When using a Wicked Edge GO sharpener, these are the lowest sharpening angles you'll be able to achieve at each measurement above the top of the vise:

- Edge rests ⅝" over top of vise—stones will clear the vise at 15 degrees per side
- Edge rests ½" over top of vise—stones will clear the vise at 17 degrees per side
- Edge rests ⅜" over top of vise—stones will clear the vise at 21 degrees per side
- Edge rests ¼" over top of vise—stones will clear the vise at 29 degrees per side

Because of these knife height limitations, sometimes you'll simply have to sharpen the knife at a wider sharpening angle. If you come across a customer who is very demanding and wants their small knife sharpened at a low angle, Wicked Edge makes a tool called the Low Angle Adapter that will help solve this issue. The Low Angle Adapter is a secondary knife clamp that clamps to the sharpener's main vise and raises the overall clamping height by one inch. It will allow you to reach approximately 5 fewer degrees of sharpening angle than you could without using it. The Low Angle Adapter was designed for clamping Japanese sushi knives, which can sometimes require sharpening angles in the range of 8 to 13 degrees per side. Though it was designed for sushi knives, it works well on small knives too. You'll find it very rare that a customer will demand a low angle on a small knife, so I don't recommend purchasing the Low Angle Adapter until you meet that specific customer.

SHARPENING FLEXIBLE KNIVES

Flexible knives can be tricky to sharpen because as you apply pressure with the stone against the knife, the knife will bend, causing the sharpening angle to change. There are a few techniques you can apply that will help prevent the knife from bending so much while you sharpen. The knife will want to bend the most as you draw the burr on one side. But, because you are only sharpening one side of the knife to draw a burr, your other hand is free, and you can use it to brace the knife. My preferred method of bracing the knife is placing my index finger against the side of the blade at the tip and placing my thumb against the side of the blade at the back of the knife. By habit, I now do this on every knife that I sharpen when I'm drawing a burr. Another benefit of bracing the knife is that you can feel if the knife starts to move in the sharpener's vise while you're drawing a burr.

Another common and effective technique to limit blade flex is to clamp the blade closer to the tip and then hold the knife's handle with one of your hands as you draw a burr with your other hand. The most flexible area of the knife is at the tip of the knife. By clamping the knife so the vise makes contact toward the tip of the blade, you can limit the flex at the tip. With the knife clamped toward the tip, the only part of the knife that needs to be controlled is the back, and holding the handle with your hand will prevent the back of the knife from flexing. This usually works out because knives that tend to be more flexible, like fillet knives, often have more curvature toward the tip of the knife and should be clamped closer to the tip anyway.

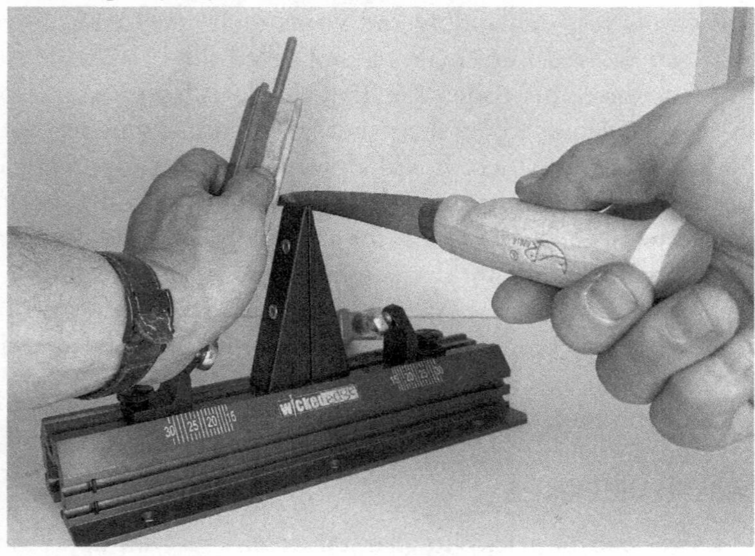

SHARPENING TECHNIQUES FOR COMMON KNIFE TYPES

CHEF'S KNIVES

The chef's knife is the most common type of knife that I sharpen. Almost every house is bound to have at least one of these. There are different sizes of chef's knives, usually ranging from six inches to twelve inches long. Though there are different sizes, the sharpening technique is the same for each size. They have a fair amount of curvature, so there is a very specific way that they should be mounted in a Wicked Edge sharpener. Clamp them so the sharpener's vise clamps the blade approximately 1.5 inches from the tip of the blade.

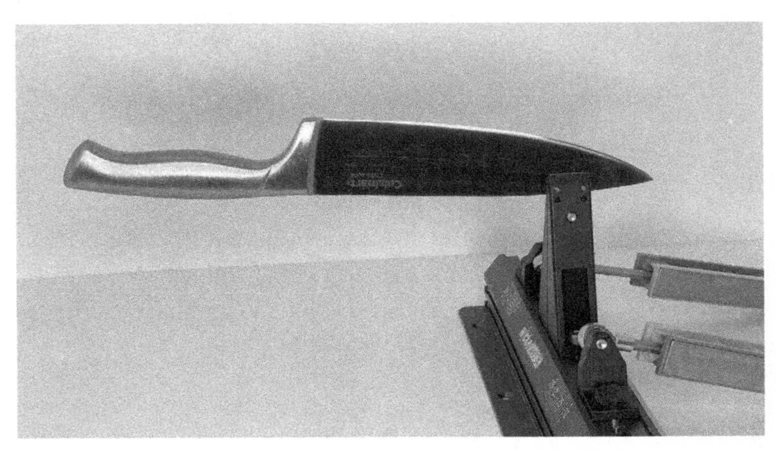

Chef's knives are usually quite sturdy, so most will not flex or bend as you apply pressure with the sharpening stones. If you do encounter a flexible one, you'll find it helpful to use a down-and-out stroke. If the blade is not flexible, you can use any stroke that you like.

FILLET KNIVES

Fillet knives are trickier to sharpen than many other blade types. The reasons that make them more complicated to sharpen are that they are very narrow, they have curvature, and they are usually flexible. They typically range in size from four inches to ten inches long. Clamp these knives as high up in the sharpener's vise as you can, but make sure the vise has a firm grip on the blade. Because of how narrow these knives are toward the tip, you may not be able to clamp them as close to the tip as they curvature might require. Clamp them as close to the tip as you can, while maintaining that the stones can clear the sharpener's vise.

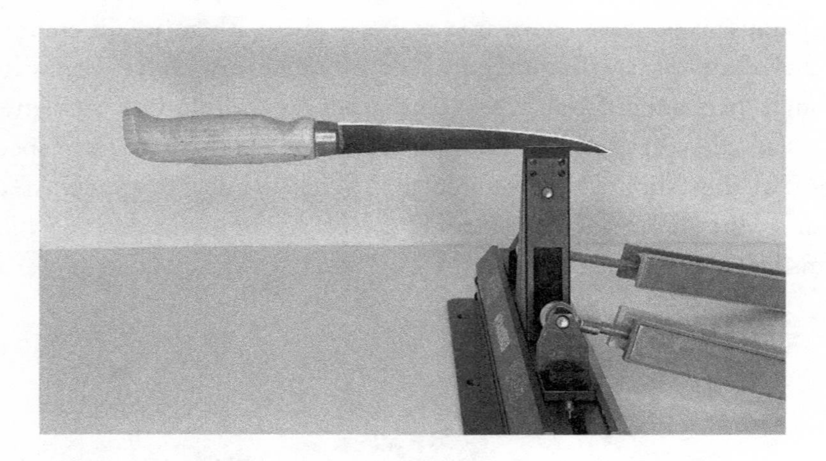

SANTOKUS

Santokus are some of the easiest knives to sharpen because they have a straight edge. They usually range in size from four inches to nine inches long. Clamp these knives so the clamp contacts the blade in the center of the blade.

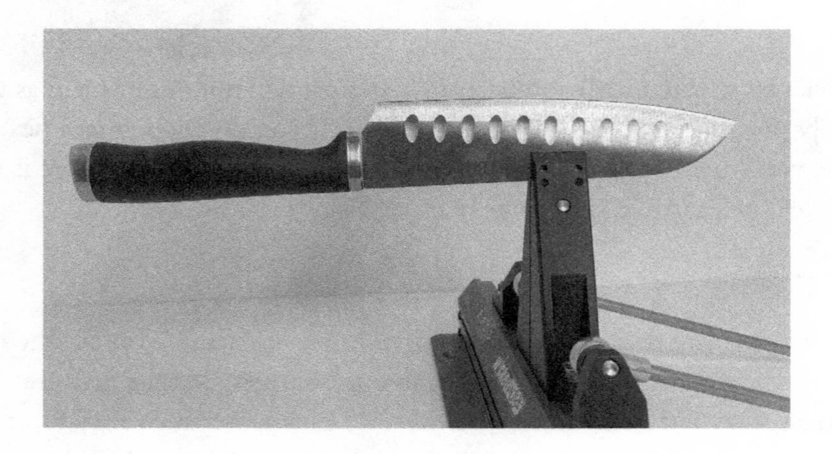

CARVING KNIVES

A carving knife is similar to a chef's knife, but it's narrower from spine to edge and doesn't have as much curvature. They usually range in size from six inches to ten inches long. Clamp these knives a little higher in the vise and so the sharpener's vise makes contact approximately 1.5 inches from the tip of the blade.

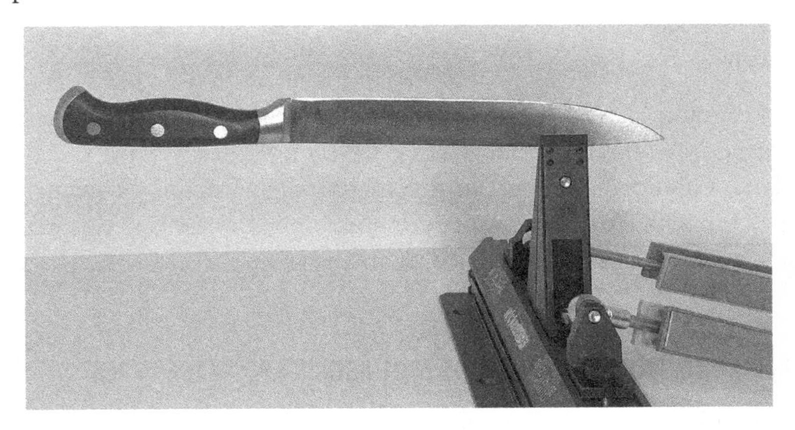

PARING KNIVES

Paring knives are small, so clamp them high in the sharpener's vise. Some have curvature, and some don't. If the knife has curvature, clamp it closer to the tip. You may need to use a wider sharpening angle to allow the stones to clear the sharpener's vise.

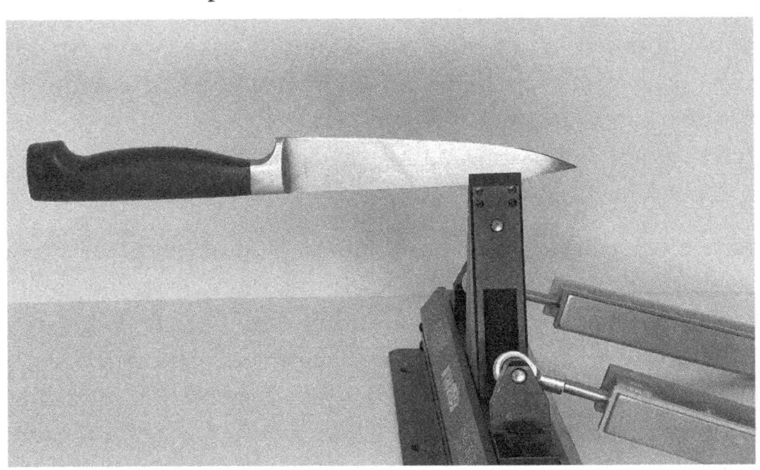

BONING KNIVES

Boning knives are small and have curvature toward the tip of the blade. Some are flexible, but most are not. Clamp them high in the sharpener's vise and clamp them so the vise contacts the knife approximately one inch away from the tip of the blade. You may need to use a wider sharpening angle to allow the stones to clear the sharpener's vise.

STEAK KNIVES

There are many different styles of steak knives. Most are on the smaller side, sometimes flexible, and usually have curvature toward the front of the blade. Clamp them high in the sharpener's vise and closer to the tip of the blade if the knife has more curvature toward the tip. You may need to use a wider sharpening angle to allow the stones to clear the sharpener's vise.

SHARPENING TECHNIQUES FOR UNIQUE EDGE GRINDS AND BLADE TYPES

Before you begin sharpening, always be on the lookout for different types of edge grinds when you examine each knife. Sometimes, the edge grind will completely change your sharpening technique. You most likely won't encounter different edge grinds very frequently, but you should know the techniques to sharpening them, so you're prepared when they cross your path.

CHISEL GRINDS

A chisel grind describes an edge that is only sharpened on one side. It is flat on the other side, just like a chisel. This type of edge grind is found most frequently on Japanese-style kitchen knives and some pocketknives. For reference, about one-one-hundredth of the knives I sharpen have a chisel grind.

The sharpening technique for these knives is quite simple. All you need to do is use the marker method to determine the sharpening angle on the side of the knife that has an edge ground into it. Then draw a burr on that side of the knife, and then progress through your various grits of stones, just like you would on any other knife. Don't touch the other side of the knife with a stone until you reach the last grit in your progression. Once you get to the last grit, there will be a burr on the flat side of the knife that will need to be knocked off. Mount your finest diamond stones onto the sharpener on both sides of the knife. Set your sharpening angle to the lowest possible angle on the flat side of the knife and leave the sharpening angle on the edged side the same as it was when you sharpened the knife. Then, make ten alternating strokes with the fine stones on both sides of the knife with very light pressure.

SCANDINAVIAN GRINDS

Scandinavian grinds, aka Scand grinds, have a very wide bevel that's ground deep into the body of the blade. When you come across one of these knives, I don't recommend trying to sharpen the entire bevel. It takes a lot of time, and any inconsistency with your stroke pressure will lead to an uneven-looking edge. Instead of trying to sharpen the whole edge, you can create a microbevel, which is a very small, secondary edge at the top of the main edge. You'll likely find that the knife probably already has a microbevel. To create or resharpen a microbevel, you'll most likely need to use a wider sharpening angle, like 25-plus degrees. Use the marker method to make sure your stones are contacting the edge's apex, and not lower down on the blade.

LARGE BLADES

Bowie knives, choppers, machetes, and small swords can all be sharpened in a Wicked Edge sharpener, and the same rules apply for sharpening them as for regular knives. If the blade has more curvature toward the tip, clamp them much closer to the tip. Because of the length of these blades, you may have difficulty touching the entire edge of the blade with a single stroke. You may have to sharpen the blade in sections. To do this, clamp the blade toward the handle first and sharpen about half the blade with all your stones. Then reclamp the blade close to the tip and sharpen the front portion with all your stones. Large blades can sometimes be heavy, and they may want to tilt in the sharpener's vise as you sharpen. Instead of overtightening your vise to grip the knives more firmly, which could be damaging to the sharpener's vise, try creating a support for the blade on either side of the sharpener. I've had success stacking books to support the blade. Wicked Edge makes longer guide rods which are compatible with any Wicked Edge sharpener model. They are not expensive. If you find yourself sharpening long blades frequently, you may consider picking up a set of longer guide rods.

DAGGERS

Dagger blades and out-the-front pocketknives often have a diamond shape. The blade is thick in the center, and tapers to form an edge on both sides of the knife. The high center point in the blade without a flat area makes these knives difficult to clamp in the sharpener. To sharpen them, make sure to use leather or moleskin in the vise, and clamp the knife so the vise makes contact with the knife closer to the tip of the blade, and so the top of the vise is positioned right onto the high centerline on the blade. These knives usually have wider sharpening angles, like 25 degrees per side or more. You'll need to sharpen one side of the knife, then flip it over and sharpen the other side of the knife. These knives will want to move in the vise as you sharpen them. Keep your eye out for knife movement, and use lighter pressure with the stones to help prevent movement. Because daggers are so tricky to sharpen, you may consider charging more for sharpening them.

SERRATED KNIVES

Serrated knives have a saw-like pattern to the edge. In the kitchen, the most common knives to have serrated edges are bread knives and steak knives. There are a number of pocketknife styles that also have serrated edges.

These knives are tricky to sharpen because flat sharpening stones do not work to sharpen them. To further complicate the issue, the patterns of the serrations are usually different from one knife to the next. Unfortunately, Wicked Edge sharpening equipment does not sharpen serrated edges. If you would like to offer sharpening services for serrated edges, you'll need additional sharpening equipment. In my opinion, the best option for sharpening serrated edges is the Spyderco Sharpmaker sharpening system. The Spyderco Sharpmaker lacks a lot of the sharpening capabilities of a Wicked Edge, like angle control, but Spyderco does make round and triangular shaped abrasive rods for their sharpening system that will fit inside and sharpen serrated patterns. If you do decide to purchase the equipment necessary to sharpen serrated knives, I recommend a lot of practice with the equipment before you offer that service to your customers.

PARTIALLY SERRATED KNIVES

Partially serrated knives have a combination of a standard flat edge and a serrated edge. Many pocketknives feature this type of edge combination, as do some steak knives.

You can use a Wicked Edge sharpener to sharpen the parts of the blade that are not serrated. Simply mount the knife in the sharpener as you would any other knife. The trick is to be cautious about how your stones touch the edge. Make sure to start your stroke so the stones don't touch the serrated portion of the blade.

Most partially serrated knives will have very different sharpening angles on one side of the knife compared to the other. Most of the time, the serrated pattern is only ground into one side of the knife. The other side of the knife is flat along the serrated portion, like a chisel grind, and has a narrow-angled edge along the nonserrated portion of the edge.

RECURVE BLADES

A recurve blade describes a knife that has an inward curve to the overall blade shape. Sometimes, this curve is steep, and other times it's quite shallow. Some knife-sharpening systems have difficulty sharpening these types of blades, but not Wicked Edge. When sharpening the majority of recurve blades, you'll find it easy to sharpen them because Wicked Edge stones have a slight radius to the corners, and they pivot 360 degrees on the guide rods. The stones will simply follow the curvature of the blade as you make your strokes. Sometimes, if the recurve is very steep, you may find it a little tricky to sharpen the knife simply because your stones won't fit into the curve. If you come across a knife that gives you trouble, you can use Wicked Edge's stone for recurve blades. These stones cost $120 for a set, so I don't recommend purchasing them until you find that you absolutely need them.

KARAMBITS, CARPET KNIVES, AND BIRD BEAKS

These knives also have a recurve shape, but to an extreme. They are shaped like a tilted crescent moon with a sharp inside edge.

When you sharpen these knives, you'll find it helpful to tilt the knife in the sharpener's vise, so the handle is upward, and the curve is level over the top of the sharpener's vise. Most of the time, you'll be able to sharpen these knives with standard Wicked Edge stones. If you can't sharpen them because the curve is too steep, you can use the stones for recurve blades.

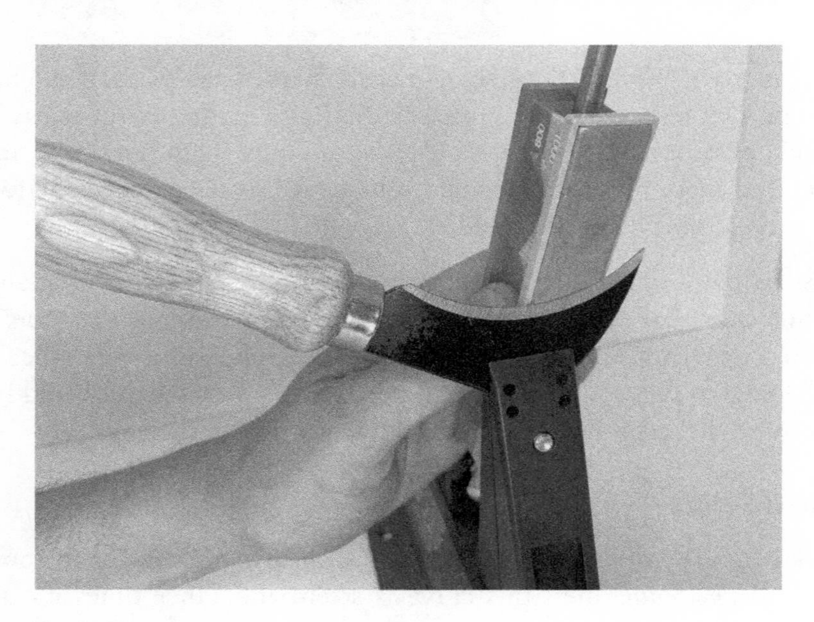

TANTO BLADES

A tanto blade has an edge that turns a sharp corner toward the point, instead of a steady slope toward the point like most knives. These types of blades are common among pocketknives and defense knives.

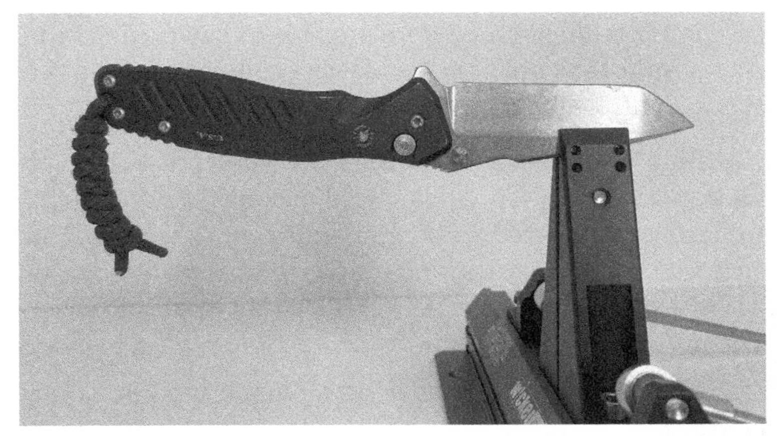

When you sharpen a tanto blade, you should treat the two areas of the edge as if they were separate edges. The sharpening angle on the forward part of the blade is almost always wider than the sharpening angle along the back part of the blade. When you use the marker method to find the angle, make sure you not only test for the angle on both sides of the blade, but also on both sections of the blade. To sharpen these types of knives, it's important to lift your stone before it turns the corner in the center of the blade. The two edges are on different planes, so the stone will want to roll over from one plane to the next. You'll be able to feel when it wants to roll as you're sharpening, and the trick is to not let it roll over the corner. Sharpen the back part of the blade first, and then readjust your angle setting and sharpen the front part of the blade. It's helpful to clamp these knives closer to the tip.

It's common that tanto blade pocketknives are also chisel ground. It's also common that they are partially serrated. Sometimes, you'll come across a tanto blade that's both chisel ground and partially serrated. I once came across a knife that had a tanto blade shape, it was partially serrated, it had a slight recurve shape along the long portion of the blade, and it was chisel ground. Knife designers just love to get creative sometimes. When you come across a blade that has multiple unique factors, just take your time and use all the necessary techniques to sharpen it correctly.

CREATING A MIRROR EDGE

If you plan to focus your sharpening service on customers who collect high-end knives, you'll need to learn how to create a mirror edge. A mirror edge is not incredibly useful for many day-to-day cutting tasks, but it sure makes a knife look great, so people who collect knives will ask you if you can put a mirror-like shine on their edges. This is how to do it.

When creating mirror-edges, the number one priority is removing scratches from the edge. You should avoid making deeper scratches in the edge, so don't use your coarser stones. Skip your 100-, 200-, and 400-grit stones and start the sharpening process with your 600-grit diamond stones. It will take you more time to reshape the edge and draw a burr, but you'll save a lot of time later in the sharpening process by not creating deeper scratches.

Use a marker to color the edge, and then determine the sharpening angle. Then draw a burr with your 600-grit stone on each side of the knife. Once you've drawn the burr, do fifty strokes on each side of the knife with your 600-grit stone.

Switch to your 800-grit diamond stone. Make fifty passes on each side using an up-and-out stroke, and then make fifty passes on each side using a down-and-out stroke. This will crisscross the scratches in the edge, which is helpful for removing them. Repeat this process with 1,000-, 1,500-, 2,200-, and 3,000-grit diamond stones.

After you've finished using all your diamond stones, switch to using Diamond Lapping Film, starting with nine microns. Make fifty passes on each side with your nine-micron Diamond Lapping Film. Always use an up-and-out stroke when using Diamond Lapping Film and use light pressure. Repeat the fifty passes with six-micron and three-micron Diamond Lapping Films.

Use a progression of leather strops to finish the edge. Start with a leather strop that has four-micron diamond emulsion on it. Do fifty passes on each side of the knife. Repeat this with three more leather strops—2, 1, and 0.5 microns.

The process of creating mirror-edges takes significantly more time than regular sharpening and requires more patience. Take your time and always be on the lookout for deeper scratches in the edge. When you see them, try to work them out using the abrasive you are currently using. Sometimes, you'll notice a deep scratch in an edge after you start stropping with leather. When that happens, it's your choice if you want to start over to remove the scratch. You know your customers, so decide if you think one scratch will annoy them. If you think it will, resharpen the knife.

MAKING REPAIRS TO KNIVES

It's very common that customers will give you knives to be sharpened that have chipped edges or broken tips. You can repair these knives using your Wicked Edge sharpening stones. If the repair is minor, I usually won't charge for it because I think it goes a long way in leaving a good impression with my customers. If the repair takes longer than ten minutes, I usually charge my customers a small fee for making the repair. If you plan to charge an additional fee for making a repair, ask your customer for permission first. Sometimes, they prefer to not pay the additional fee and will be upset with you if you don't give them the choice.

CHIPPED EDGES

Edges become chipped when the knife hits something hard in the process of cutting, like bone, or when a knife is dropped or banged into something. Some chips are very minor and require little effort to repair. Others can be deep, requiring much more work. To repair chipped blades, mount the knife in the knife sharpener to stabilize it. Then, take your 100-grit diamond stone and place it straight down onto the edge of the knife. Push the stone forward and backward along the edge as many times as you need to, until the chips are gone. Make sure the stone touches the entire length of the edge with each pass. Don't just work on the area of the knife that has the chip; otherwise, low spots in the edge will form and the edge will come out wavy. I highly recommend wearing cut-proof gloves when you remove chips from an edge. After the chips have been removed, sharpen the knife using the regular sharpening process. You'll find it more difficult to draw a burr than normal, because of the material you've removed from the edge.

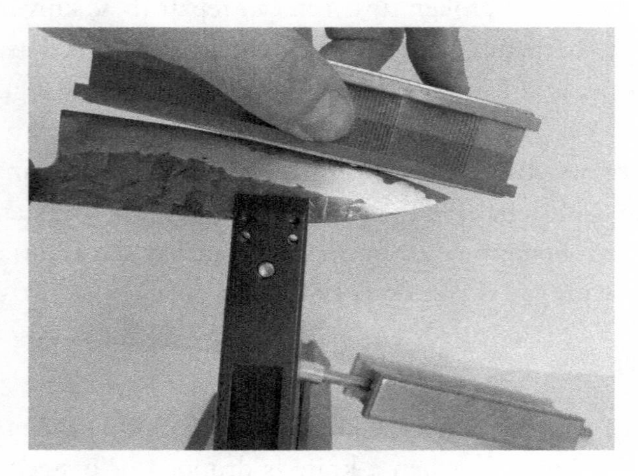

BROKEN TIPS

Tips often break off knives when knives are dropped or misused. To repair a broken tip, remove metal from the knife until a new tip is formed. You can remove metal from the edged side of the knife, or from the spine of the knife. I prefer a combination of both. The process is like fixing chips. Mount the knife in the sharpener and then run the 100-grit diamond stone back and forth along either the edge or the spine at the front of the blade until a new tip is formed. If you would like to remove metal from the spine of the knife, clamp the knife in the sharpener upside down. Again, I highly recommend wearing a cut-proof glove when you're making this repair. Some broken tips are very minor and easily repaired. Sometimes, a large portion of the front of the knife has broken off, and it can take twenty minutes or more to repair. Once the knife has a new tip, sharpen the knife using the regular sharpening process. You'll find it more difficult to draw a burr than normal, owing to the material you've removed from the edge.

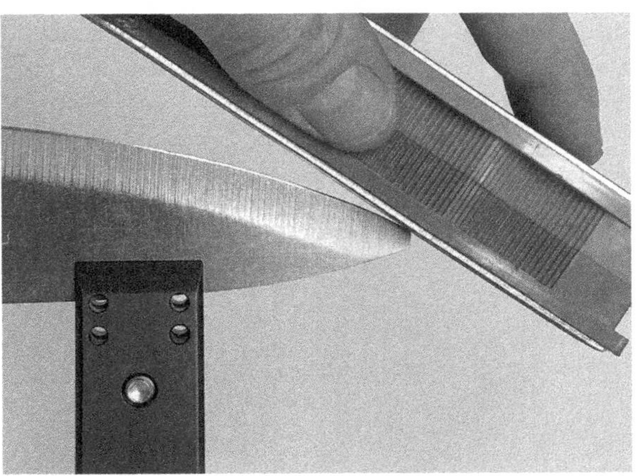

BENT TIPS

Every time I have ever tried to repair a bent tip, it always ends poorly. The tip usually breaks off the knife when I try to bend it back into place. For this reason, I do not recommend attempting to fix bent tips unless you have blacksmithing or blade-forging capabilities.

TAKE YOUR TIME

If you're taking your time and paying close attention to what you are doing, you can figure out how to sharpen any knife. Because Wicked Edge is a manual system, you can make detailed observations about what's happening as you sharpen, and then adjust accordingly. When you first start using the sharpener, don't feel like you need to rush. When learning any new skill, it's much more important to develop good habits than it is to try to rush to good results. Go slowly and pay close attention and think about every action you take. The speed will come with practice. Remember: protecting your customers' knives is your top priority, and achieving excellent results is a close second.

My final piece of advice about sharpening is this: take pride in your work. After you sharpen each knife, test the edge for sharpness, and then say to yourself, *I did that.* Your business won't work unless you take pride in what you do and share that pride with the people around you. When you sharpen knives and deliver them, your customers will often check the edge for sharpness in front of you. It's an awesome feeling to see their faces and reactions when they see just how sharp you made their knives. Take mental notes of those moments to keep for yourself.

CHAPTER 11

YOU'RE NOT ON YOUR OWN

Many people who choose to start businesses do so because they have a background or an expertise in the field of the business they choose to create. If you're considering knife sharpening as a business for yourself, and you don't have experience with knives or sharpening, it may feel intimidating. From what you've learned in this book, you'll be able to start a knife-sharpening service and operate it successfully. However, there may be times when you need to ask a question or run an idea by someone in the industry. In addition to the resources at my website, startasharpeningservice.com, there are tons of other resources available. These online forums are excellent if you have questions about specific knives or how to sharpen them. I recommend creating an account on all three of the below forums so you can interact with other people and ask questions.

Wicked Edge Forum: https://knife.wickededgeusa.com/

Blade Forums: https://www.bladeforums.com/

Kitchen Knife Forums: https://www.kitchenknifeforums.com/

If you would like to learn more about the knife industry, including current industry news, I highly recommend subscribing to *Blade* magazine. You can visit its website at https://blademag.com/.

In addition to its publication, *Blade* magazine also hosts the International Blade Show and Cutlery Fair. There are two shows every year. The main show, which takes place in Atlanta at the beginning of June, is an amazing place to meet with knife makers and other people involved in the industry, check out all the latest sharpening and knife-making equipment, and learn all there is to learn about knives. It's a wonderful event. I believe the Blade Show represents the heartbeat of the knife industry. If you can't make it to Atlanta, there is a second Blade Show that takes place in Portland in the fall.

Many companies offer training to help people become familiar with how to use their services. If you need help building your website, understanding how to use QuickBooks, or need a brush-up on Microsoft Office, you'll find plenty of online resources to help you. All of the resources listed below are free.

- **Wix Training Academy:**
https://www.wixtrainingacademy.com/
- **Squarespace Online Training:**
https://circle.squarespace.com/online-courses
- **QuickBooks Training:**
https://quickbookstraining.com/
- **Microsoft Office Training:**
https://support.microsoft.com/en-us/training
- **Google Business Training:**
https://grow.google/
- **Google Analytics Academy:**
https://analytics.google.com/analytics/academy
- **Facebook Marketing Training:**
https://www.facebook.com/business/learn

While you're getting your business started, and afterward, there will be times when you become frustrated. You may not have the answer to a question a customer asks, or you may become flustered because a knife is proving incredibly difficult to sharpen. I don't think anyone who's ever started a business, especially their first business, hasn't experienced frustration points or learning curves that they had to overcome. But that's exactly what happens—you will learn and overcome your challenges. Try to embrace your frustration points as learning opportunities, because it's at these moments that we push the boundaries of our minds and capabilities, and we grow. You're about to do something wonderful for yourself, so let the small worries and doubts go, and trust yourself to overcome your obstacles. It won't be long before your business practically runs itself, and all you need to do is show up on time, sharpen knives, and delight your customers with your amazing service. And remember, owning a business isn't all work. It's also incredibly rewarding, and it's a lot of fun. I wish you the best of luck!

CPSIA information can be obtained
at www.ICGtesting.com
Printed in the USA
LVHW100410220822
726519LV00003B/233